Sisters and Brothers

Sisters and Brothers

Resolving Your Adult Sibling Relationships

PATTI McDERMOTT, M.F.C.C.

LOWELL HOUSE
Los Angeles
CONTEMPORARY BOOKS
Chicago

Library of Congress Cataloging-in-Publication Data

McDermott, Patti.
    Sisters and brothers: resolving your adult sibling relationships / Patti McDermott.
       p.   cm.
    Includes bibliographical references and index.
    ISBN 0-929923-56-1
    1. Sisters and brothers. 2. Sibling rivalry. 3. Adulthood—Psychological aspects. I. Title.
BF723.S43M453 1992
158'.24—dc20
                                  92-18827
                                       CIP

Requests for such permissions should be addressed to:
Lowell House
2029 Century Park East, Suite 3290
Los Angeles, CA 90067

Publisher: Jack Artenstein
Executive Vice-President: Nick Clemente
Vice-President/Editor-in-Chief: Janice Gallagher
Design: Nancy Freeborn

Manufactured in the United States of America
10 9 8 7 6 5 4 3 2 1

All happy families are like one another;
each unhappy family is unhappy in its own way.
—Leo Tolstoy

Contents

Acknowledgments

I wish to thank:

All my clients past and present, for allowing me the privilege of sharing their lives and, in the process, teaching me so much about sibling relationships.

Janice Gallagher, for her interest in the book from the very beginning, her constant flow of exciting ideas, her support and encouragement, and finally, for trusting that I would find my own way even when I doubted I could.

Betsy Amster, for teaching me how to form the structure to support my thoughts, for her patience, intelligence, and terrific sense of humor, and for sharing her ideas and always challenging mine.

Molly Maguire Silverman, for coming into this project at a difficult time and handling the transition with sensitivity, for her good suggestions and help in tying the book together in its last stages.

Beverly Engel, my dear friend, for suggesting I write this book in the first place, convincing me I could do it, and paving the way for me at Lowell House, and for her loving friendship.

Kim Boroczi, for all her research runs to the UCLA library, as well as her support and continuing interest in my projects.

Eddie Arkin, Linda Barnes, Scott Boroczi, Susan Cox, Patricia Feiner, Alan Fox, Marty Josephson, and Mary Miotto, for their belief in me, their support, and their feedback. Patricia, a special thanks for taking the time to listen to my questions and giving me good answers to all of them.

Dylan McDermott Boroczi, for sleeping through the night, which made it possible for me to write during the day.

Sheryl Strauss, for her excellent copy editing.

Peter Hoffman, for his sensitive and efficient handling of my manuscript, and for always taking the time to answer my questions.

Bud Sperry, for his marketing skills as well as keeping me informed and entertained.

Everyone at Lowell House who helped make this book happen.

Introduction

From the beginning of my work as a psychotherapist, I've applied what I've learned about my own sibling relationships to my work with clients. Because of this focus, I've been asked over and over again how I became a "sibling therapist." In fact I am not a sibling therapist—no therapist can afford to focus on only one aspect of a client's life—but I do pay more attention than most to the sibling relationship and the impact it has on people's lives.

My own early experiences with my siblings played an enormous part in forming my identity as an adult, and I discovered that the same was true for many of my clients and their siblings. The sibling relationship is one of the most profound and complex of all relationships, yet it is largely ignored in the therapeutic environment. It was the lack of information, support, and respect for the value of working through this important relationship that compelled me to write *Sisters and Brothers*.

Clients rarely come to see me specifically for help with a sibling problem. As a matter of course, however, I probe into their relationships with their brothers and sisters as thoroughly as I probe into their relationships with their parents, because I realize how important sibling interactions can be. Perhaps a bit of my own history will help to explain what I mean:

I grew up thinking that my older sister, Joanne, was special while I was ordinary. Joanne, the first grandchild on both sides, was labeled the beauty of the family. Where I was quiet, shy, and watchful, she was vivacious, mischievous, and funny. Whenever there was a family gathering, my sister was in the middle of the action, while I was somewhere in the background, fading into the woodwork.

Joanne and I might well have become enemies, but because of the chaos within our family (our mother had emotional problems, our father had a drinking problem), she became my protector and friend. I admired her, believed what everyone said about her, and willingly followed her lead.

Both Joanne and I were very protective toward our brother, Harry, born nine years after me, and Harry in turn counted on his big sisters to provide stability and a feeling of safety. He worried a lot about our parents and, because of his asthma, he fell behind in school. All of us, my parents, my sister, and I, took to referring to him as "poor Harry."

So there we were: poor Harry, chipper Joanne, and mousy Patti, three siblings imprisoned in roles we grew to hate well before we reached adulthood.

When I was in my mid-twenties an incident occurred that made me realize just how different the adult Harry was from the child Harry. After he had a motorcycle accident, Joanne and I went to visit our brother and found his room so full of people that we had to push our way in to say hello. The room was decorated with balloons, and there were get-well cards everywhere. From his bed, his face radiant with health, he waved a pen at us and pointed to his cast; there was barely any room left for our signatures. It was startling to realize that gradually, over the years, my brother had grown into someone I didn't know.

A similar jolt happened when my future husband met Joanne for the first time. After the evening was over and we were driving home, I was extolling her virtues to George when he said quietly, "Yes, she's all those things, but so are you, in your own way."

I instantly got angry. "Well, that's not the point. I wasn't talking about myself, I was talking about Joanne," I shot back.

"But you're doing what everybody else in your family does," George replied. "You're talking about her as if she's superhuman or something. I mean, I liked her, I liked her a lot. But you've got a problem about her."

We rode the rest of the way home in silence, and in that silence the truth washed over me: For years, I had covered up my envious feelings by saying all kinds of wonderful things about Joanne before anyone else had the chance. It hurt less if all the accolades came from me instead of from everybody else in my family. That night I realized for the first time that no matter how close, loyal, and loving Joanne and I were, those early years and outside forces had affected me and our relationship.

The next day I drove back to my sister's. The thought of talking to her about what I was feeling was frightening, because another revelation I had had the night before was that we had *never* talked about ourselves with each other. Although I trusted Joanne with my life and I knew she would trust me with hers, we had always focused on the problems in our family, not our own feelings.

When I arrived, I took a deep breath and told Joanne how much I had envied her while growing up and how bad I had felt when everyone doted on her and ignored me.

To my surprise, Joanne replied that she had always felt great pressure to be "on" and had always *envied me.* I was so self-assured, she said, so self-contained that I didn't need anyone else's attention. "You just did your own thing, Patti, and I really envied that."

"Oh no," I said. "I was too terrified to pipe up like you did. I was terrified of being visible."

After that exchange, we stared at each other in amazement. It was as if we were seeing each other for the first time. "You know, I actually have a good sense of humor, just like you do," I told Joanne. "And I'm capable of being as serious as you are," she replied with a smile. We realized that those sides of our personalities—my sense of humor, Joanne's seriousness—had not been allowed expression because they were counter to the roles we each played in our family.

Over the years, as Joanne and I have worked to get to know each other, both of our personalities have expanded. Now, for instance, at family functions and elsewhere, Joanne can be reflective and quiet, just as I can be outgoing and funny. Also, the focus of our relationship has shifted dramatically. Whereas before we talked solely of problems in our family of origin, now we share our lives and talk about *our feelings* about the past. In the process we've healed not only our relationship with each other but also our relationship with our parents. Now the history we shared enriches our present relationship but doesn't overwhelm it.

With Harry, I had to let go, finally, of seeing him as my little brother who needed my help. Today I treat Harry like the adult he is, and he sees me as a person who has problems like anyone else, rather than as an omnipotent older sister.

You, too, may be in for as many or more surprises as I had when you examine your sibling relationship closely. Although it is not easy to leave behind the view you hold of yourself and your sibling from childhood, it's well worth the effort, as you'll understand while reading this book. Discovering who your sibling is today will enable you to pull your relationship with him or her into the present and will carry you into the future—together.

CHAPTER ONE

Risks and Rewards

The sibling relationship goes to the core of our identities. Although as children we are all dependent upon our parents for survival, it is often our siblings off whom we bounce our identity issues in our early years. For instance, a popular older brother may have more power than a father to devastate the confidence of a shy younger sister who is getting ready to go out on her first date. Or an older sister can be demoralized when a younger brother eclipses her achievements, then taunts her about his success.

I have seen time and again with my clients how their early interactions with siblings continue to affect their lives as adults. Having grown up together, most siblings find it difficult to recognize each other as adults and to leave behind their frozen childhood images of each other.

But a magical transformation occurs when siblings suddenly start to really talk to each other after many years. I've seen it many times by now, but the power of the emotions continues to impress me. Even if those first words are angry or resentful or full of past hurts, the moment still has enormous power; it's like seeing a glacier move.

A SIMPLE QUIZ

Take a moment to answer the following questions:

Do you have unexplained feelings of anger or resentment toward your sibling?

Are you anxious, critical, or disapproving if your sibling doesn't do what he or she is "supposed" to do?

Do you feel your sibling is hogging all the attention?

Do you see yourself as the opposite of your sibling?

Do you gauge your achievements against those of your sibling?

Have you given up certain activities because your sibling is better at them?

Is your relationship still based on trying to best each other?

Is what happens to your sibling more important than what happens to you?

Do you feel angry at or jealous of your sibling because he has done well in something that is difficult for you?

Are you angry at your sibling for getting special treatment from your parents?

Do you wish your younger sibling would "grow up"?

Do you wish your older sibling would take you seriously?

Do you wish you could talk to your sibling but don't know how?

Are you still afraid of a sibling who abused you as a child?

Are you still being abused—physically, emotionally, or sexually—by a sibling?

Do you blame your sibling for the problems in your relationship?

If you answered yes to even one of these questions, you will find *Sisters and Brothers* helpful in laying to rest your conflicts with your sibling.

Of course, the process of bringing your childhood conflicts into the open and resolving them as adults may hurt, especially as past injuries resurface. But you will also gain a tremendous sense of relief and a new feeling of family. "It's been a real pleasure to get to know my sister," I've been told again and again. Or, "I feel like I've regained my brother. I never thought we'd get past the rivalry that ruined our relationship as kids, but we have." I've seen many clients, whose sibling relationships were filled with anger and bitterness over old hurts, rivalries, and misunderstandings, learn to have close, trusting, loving relationships.

You, too, can turn your relationships around and resolve old battles, complaints, and misconceptions. As you'll see in the chapters that follow, what it takes is a willingness to:

• see your sibling as well as yourself through fresh eyes.

• let go of blame and resentment and listen to what your sibling has to say.

• let go of old roles.

• make a commitment to be honest with your sibling and yourself about your feelings.

• be open to change.

• nurture a relationship with your siblings apart from your relationship with your parents.

• deal with family issues that you may not have faced yet, including sibling or parental sexual abuse.

• pick up the phone and say, "Let's talk, I miss you."

The Wider World

Both parental and sibling relationships are what therapists call source relationships, or those that influence who we become. We carry the history of such relationships into the world with us, and in many ways they determine the relationships we have as adults.

If your sibling relationship has been problematic and you haven't yet worked it out, then not only will that relationship be frozen, but the relationships you develop later in life will get stuck in the same spots. Holding onto resentment, anger, jealousy, awe, undeserved loyalty, or fear will undermine your current relationships and make it impossible for you to experience them fully in the present.

If you suspect that the problems between you and your sibling are affecting your other relationships, take a moment to answer these questions:

Do you find yourself being a "big sister" or "big brother" to other people in your life?

Do you like telling your co-workers and friends what to do, but then have difficulty asking for help or trusting others' judgments?

Do you feel resentful or angry around others who seem to be getting more attention than you are?

Do you bully people who remind you of your younger siblings?

Do you feel like everyone tells you what to do, just as your older brother or sister did?

Do you ask for or expect your co-workers, spouse, or friends to make excuses for you?

Are you a people pleaser?

Do you concede certain areas of expertise to others based on how you and your sibling were labeled in your family?

Do you back away from competitive situations because you were always bested by your sibling at home?

Do you involve yourself in relationships that mimic your abusive relationship with a sibling?

Do you treat your children as your parents treated you and your sibling?

Do you favor one of your children over the others?

Do you get angry and abusive with your children, just as you and your sibling behaved with each other?

Do you avoid people who remind you of your brother or sister?

When it comes to your siblings, the conflicts you avoid and the feelings you bury are the very ones most likely to come back to haunt you in your other relationships. By working out your relationship with your siblings, you will learn to recognize and avoid destructive patterns. You will be more in control of your reactions to your partner, your children, your boss, your colleagues, and your friends.

Have You Married Your Sibling?

When a source relationship is left unfinished or unresolved, we tend to repeat it over and over again in our other relationships in an effort to work it out. This is what Freud referred to as the repetition compulsion. What this means in practice is that just as many of us "marry" our siblings as "marry" our parents.

They may not realize it, but often people choose a mate who reminds them of a brother or sister. This happened to my client Susan. Her older brother, Hal, was a favored child good in everything: sports, academics, social occasions. Her parents didn't hide their pride in their son, and they made no effort to find out what was special about Susan.

Susan's way of handling the favoritism was to move out of the house as soon as she was able and to have barely any contact with Hal. He was a nice guy, she told me, who tried to be friends with her, but it was simply too painful for her to respond to his overtures of friendship. "I'm tired of walking around feeling unworthy and stupid, and it all started with my brother," she told me. "I even married a guy just like him whom I could feel inadequate around and resentful of," she added.

The instant the words came out she sat up, shocked. She had never made this connection between her brother and her husband before. "I'll be damned if I didn't go and *marry* my brother, and here I am talking about how I avoided him all these years."

Sometimes people marry someone like their sibling to maintain their comfort zone. For instance, Jeff was the tag-along younger brother of his sister Marilyn, who was outgoing and popular. He ended up marrying a woman with a similar personality, someone who continued to pave the way for him, who didn't pressure him to go out and make his own friends.

By continuing a pattern such as this with a spouse, you are depriving yourself of the opportunity to expand your own personality. You are choosing instead to play the same safe role that you had vis-à-vis your brother or sister.

Have You Let Your Sibling Relationship Determine Your Friendships?

Most of us want siblings; if we don't have them—or don't like the ones we have—we try to re-create brothers or sisters with friends. Often people give up on their sibling relationships or accept their limitations because they don't know how to begin to change them. Instead, they try to create their ideal sibling relationship with someone else.

But the problems you had with your siblings will almost certainly crop up in your friendships as well, no matter how much you wish these new relationships to be different. If you have been in awe of an older brother, for instance, you may find it difficult to have balanced relationships with men friends. If you avoid your sister because she's always telling you what to do, you're probably also avoiding other people like her. If your brother needed your help all the time, you may end up with friends who are needy and dependent.

All of these friendships will leave you feeling angry, hurt, lonely, or misunderstood. These feelings may be subtle or pronounced, but if you don't acknowledge that you have a particular problem with your sibling, you will not recognize the same pattern in your friendships, or you will recognize it but be helpless to change it.

For many years, I was drawn to women friends who were outgoing, very attractive, and full of fun—life-of-the-party types. I thought I was perfectly happy to be in the background, but occasionally I would feel resentful and angry at their "big egos" or their "need to be noticed." My resentment would soon turn to dissatisfaction with myself. What was wrong with me? Why didn't people pay attention to me? Why did I have to be so quiet?

Then I discovered that I had been covering up my feelings of resentment and jealousy toward my sister for being labeled the pretty, lively one. When I talked to her about these feelings, my friendships with women changed dramatically. This "working through" freed me to develop friendships based on mutual interests, affection, and respect, not on a compulsion to replay the hurtful aspects of my relationship with my sister. Moreover, it finally forced me to take responsibility for myself socially.

Do You Cart Your Sibling Along with You to Work?

The same repetition compulsion holds true for work relationships; they often repeat the power dynamics of a sibling relationship. For instance, the youngest sibling in a family may have an easier time taking orders from a boss than does an older sibling who was accustomed to being in charge at home.

Marilyn's older sister, Penny, was bossy and most of the time treated

Marilyn as if she were stupid. As a child, she would watch for Marilyn to make a mistake, then pounce on the chance to point out yet again how incapable Marilyn was. Marilyn was intimidated by Penny, so her way of handling the relationship was to avoid her sister as much as possible.

As an adult, Marilyn constantly had trouble at work. She was overly sensitive to criticism; she would either quit in embarrassed defeat if she sensed that anyone was unhappy with her, or she'd fly into a rage and attack anyone who dared to say anything about her work. Needless to say, she had few friends on the job. People avoided her, and although she was hurt by her isolation, she felt helpless to change. After all the years of listening to her sister's criticisms, Marilyn had built up a tremendous rage, and her co-workers and bosses were the victims of it.

Marilyn eventually told her sister her feelings and thereafter demanded that Penny treat her with respect. She developed the response of walking out of the room the instant Penny said anything critical. Gradually their relationship shifted, and so, too, did Marilyn's work relationships.

"I feel free now," she said. "I'm still sensitive to criticism, but it's manageable, I can handle it. I know that most people aren't out to get me like Penny. She just wanted to jab me all the time; now I realize there is such a thing as constructive criticism and that I can't expect myself to do everything right the first time out."

Do You Replay Your Sibling Relationship with Your Children?

People tend to repeat their own sibling relationships with their children. Children who grow up in homes marked by favoritism or unhealthy competition, for instance, often pass these same problems on to the next generation.

For example, my client David grew up in a highly competitive atmosphere with his siblings. When his two kids were very young, David found himself egging them on to compete with each other by saying such things as, "Your brother was already out of diapers by this age," or "Even your sister can run faster than you."

Counseling helped David to understand the damage done to his relationship with his brother and sister through his parents' emphasis on competition. By working through the competitive feelings he still experienced toward his own siblings, David was able to stop repeating this pattern with his children.

Working out your sibling relationships requires that you understand how your family operates. If you can penetrate the labyrinth of your own complex family—for all family relationships are intricate and multilayered—you can work through anything. Once you understand your reactions to your siblings, as well as their reactions to you and where those reactions are coming from, you are on your way to being able to understand the complexities of almost any relationship. If you can break through all the old barriers with your sibling, I believe you will be able to conquer any new relationship that comes your way.

What You'll Learn by Reading This Book

The most common sibling problems I encounter in my practice are derived from favoritism, competition, birth order, parental expectations, parental needs, parental conflicts, labeling, and emotional, sexual, and verbal abuse. Chapters in this book discuss each of these issues. Let me note here that, while I've included many case histories in *Sisters and Brothers,* I have taken care to disguise my clients' identities to preserve their privacy.

The seeds for problematic sibling relationships are sown in early childhood. In Chapter Two, Great Expectations: How Parents Set the Stage for Troubled Sibling Relationships, you will gain a clearer understanding of the way your parents' needs shaped your relationship with your brother or sister.

The older/younger sibling roles are embedded in our sibling relationships from the outset. In Chapter Three, "I'm Not Your Little Brother Anymore!": Equalizing Sibling Relationships, you will learn how to free yourself from the burden of an unequal sibling relationship.

Chapter Four, "You're the Intelligent One, and Your Sister Is the Pretty One": Getting Beyond Parental Labels, will help you gain the freedom to expand your personality into areas you've always thought your sibling had locked up. Chapter Five, "Mom Always Liked You Best": Overcoming the Legacy of Favoritism, will help you learn how to counter the ill effects of any favoritism your parents may have shown to your sibling or to you.

Competition is often one of the most divisive influences on the sibling relationship. Chapter Six, "I'll Never Be as Successful as My Brother": Resolving Competitive Feelings, will give you the understanding you need to mend a highly rivalrous relationship with a brother or sister.

Many siblings find themselves caught up in their parents' conflicts. In reading Chapter Seven, The Parent-Sibling Vise: Stepping Out from Between Your Parents, you will learn how to develop a separate relationship with your sibling that no longer revolves around your parents' problems.

Of course, not all siblings live happily ever after. Some relationships are so destructive that it is a sign of emotional health to end them. Chapter Eight, "I've Never Been Able to Stand Up to Him": Coming to Terms with Violence and Neglect; and Chapter Nine, "We Couldn't Talk About It": Facing the Trauma of Sexual Abuse and Incest, show how many of my clients managed to pull away once and for all from a sibling who abused them physically or sexually. These chapters provide plenty of suggestions for you to use if you are in a similar situation.

Once you are on the road to resolving conflicts and opening the lines of communication between you and your sibling, you can pass what you have learned on to the next generation. Chapter Ten, Moving into the Future: Helping Your Children Form Healthy Sibling Relationships, focuses on how to help your own children create healthy relationships with each other.

Working out your sibling relationship requires that you understand how your family operated when you were a child and how it operates now. This takes effort, but if you can work your way through a troubled relationship with a brother or sister, you can work through any new relationship as well. Many of the clients whose stories I tell in these pages found added benefits from improving a sibling relationship. They gained the ability to work with people they never thought they could work with because they were too reminiscent of a brother or sister. They found they could befriend people they never thought they could relate to.

Once you forge a healthy adult relationship with your sibling, you'll be in a much better position to cooperate in helping your aging parents—without squabbling. Difficult as it may be to contemplate, you'll also find it much easier to cope together with the death of a parent.

By resolving your childhood relationship with your sibling and bringing it into the present, you also have the potential for a lifelong friendship with a person who knows you perhaps better than anyone else. Once you've put your long-standing conflicts to rest, you'll be able to share your joint history without rancor and old resentments getting in the way. You'll find support and understanding for mutual problems. You'll have someone to share your accomplishments and joy with. You'll also be in a position to learn from each other by sharing your different perceptions of your family of origin. What could be more rewarding than sitting down with your sibling and openly talking about how you felt about each other and your family while you were growing up?

CHAPTER TWO

Great Expectations

How Parents Set the Stage for Troubled Sibling Relationships

We are all familiar with the notion that married couples bring their parents with them into their relationship, but few siblings recognize that they do the same. In fact, the saying "It's bigger than both of us" applies at least as much to siblings as it does to lovers. Your current feelings for a sibling may have been programmed into your relationship even before you were born. Some of the fights that seem an inevitable part of your life with your brother or sister probably didn't originate with you, but may be a legacy inherited from your parents.

For many siblings who don't get along, the effort to uncover the parental expectations that shaped their relationship is like solving a puzzle. Once the pieces fall into place, life makes more sense. Discovering that the problems you've always had with each other aren't all your fault brings with it the welcome possibility of change.

Parental expectations carry a lot of power because they are driven by parental needs: "I need someone to win for me so that I can feel good about myself." "I need children who will do for me what I can't do for myself." "I need us to be one big happy family." Of course, not all parents expect their children to be a certain way, but if your parents did, by putting their needs ahead of yours they determined the way your sibling relationship would develop.

Children are always tuned in to their parents' needs. Whether your parents' expectations were spoken or implied made no difference; if the message you got from them was, "I need you to save me," you did everything you could to meet that need. As a child you were dependent on your parents for your survival, and the thought of losing them was terrifying. The stakes were high—if you failed, your ultimate terror might materialize: your parents wouldn't love you or would abandon you. If you succeeded, you hoped your parents would stay put.

The fear of not being loved or of being abandoned, physically or emotionally, is a profound one for children. Even if your parents' expectations were destructive to you or to your relationship with your siblings, you undoubtedly tried to fulfill their expectations out of the fear of abandonment. Now you find yourself in a role that doesn't permit you and your siblings to see each other fully.

Once you discover what expectations your parents had of you and your sibling, you can explore the effects of these expectations on your relationship. You may need to be a bit of a sleuth to ferret out what you need to know, but it's well worth the effort.

If you answer yes to any of the following questions, then your relationship with your sibling may be at least partially based on your parents' expectations:

Do you have unexplained feelings of anger or resentment toward your sibling?

Are you anxious, critical, or disapproving if your sibling doesn't do what he or she is "supposed" to do?

Are you determined not to like your sibling, no matter what?

Do you feel that your sibling never gave you a chance?

Do you worry about whether you and your sibling are making your parents happy?

Do you have a family secret that is kept from the world?

Are you or one of your siblings working to satisfy your parents' dream?

Do you pressure your sibling to be a better son or daughter to your parents?

EXERCISE

Take a piece of paper and write out the following sentences, filling in the blanks for yourself:

"My parents expected me to be_____."

"My parents expected my brother/sister to be_____."

Try to write at least 10 expectations your parents had of you and of your sibling. These might include things like, "My parents expected me to be polite/studious/perfect/a mother to my sister/part of the family myth/dependent/independent."

Then write on another piece of paper:

"I expected my brother/sister to be_____."

"My brother/sister expected me to be_____."

Again write at least 10 expectations for each statement. These might include statements such as, "I expected my brother to be needy/fragile/dependent/good/cute/funny/strong/independent."

How Parents Script Sibling Relationships

Do your expectations of your sibling dovetail with your parents' expectations? Are your expectations of your sibling unreasonable or unfair? Do your expectations of your sibling focus on pleasing your parents? If your answer to any of these questions is yes, this is a clue that your parents scripted your relationship. Now that you're an adult, you can seize the opportunity to rewrite the script. The following anecdotes will illustrate some of the different types of parental expectations and how they impact on the sibling relationship.

"If It Weren't for You, I'd Go Crazy All Alone in This House": Parents' Differing Expectations

Parents, like everybody else, are constantly changing. Their needs vary depending on many factors: their relationship with each other, their emotional health, their maturity, their finances. These shifting needs often explain why parents expect one set of behaviors from their first child and another from later children.

Vacillating expectations can have a profound influence on the sibling relationship. For instance, if your parents were struggling financially when they had you, they may not have been able to buy you many clothes or toys. If their finances improved and your brother got everything his little heart desired when he came along five years later, you probably ended up feeling jealous and angry at him.

Norma originally came to see me in therapy because she was mistrustful of people and had a difficult time sustaining relationships with both men and women. She was insecure and suspicious of other people's motives. She mistrusted every new employee at her office and worried that someone else would usurp her position.

After a brief discussion of her family history, I suggested that Norma would benefit from going back to her source relationships to help her make sense of her life. She quickly discovered that the differing expectations her parents had for her and for her brother set the stage for many of the problems they had with each other as well as many of the problems she was having in other relationships.

Norma's parents moved from their hometown in the Midwest to California soon after they got married. They had no friends or family in Los Angeles, and Norma's father's work required a lot of travel the first few years. Norma was conceived to help ease her mother's loneliness. When Norma was little her mother would pick her up, squeeze her tight, and whisper fiercely, "If it weren't for you, I would go crazy all alone in this house."

By the time her brother, Leonard, was born five years later, Norma was accustomed to spending a lot of time with her mother and had grown to feel special and important in her mother's life. She had also felt the burden of her mother's loneliness and had done her best to make her mother happy. In the five years after Norma's birth, her mother had made a lot of friends, and Norma always went along when her mother went visiting. But suddenly baby Leonard was being displayed and cooed over up and down the street, while Norma was sent off to school for the first time. Understandably, Norma hated Leonard for ruining her life.

Leonard was conceived because Norma's mother thought it was time to have another child, and she wanted a boy. When Leonard came along she delighted in his "strength" and "independence," and soon she was criticizing Norma for her "clinginess" and jealousy.

Because their mother didn't need Leonard to assuage her loneliness, she allowed him more freedom than she had Norma. As they grew older, Norma perceived Leonard's freedom as neglect of their parents. "He's a conniving, selfish person who doesn't care about anybody but himself and his friends," she said to me.

Later when I met Leonard, he told me, "Norma has always hated me, for as long as I can remember." His memory of his sister in the early years was of someone he was always trying to win over. "She was just so contemptuous of me; she had no use for a little brother. I guess I learned early to be independent."

Before these two children were born, their mother's needs—for a companion in Norma's case and for a brave, independent son in Leonard's—had already defined their relationship. Over the years, Norma continued to see Leonard as an intruder, and Leonard continued to view Norma as distant and unapproachable. As adults, Leonard and Norma simply didn't know each other.

As Norma sorted through her relationship with her brother in therapy, she felt sad at how little she really knew about him. The more she realized that her feelings about him were based on factors over which neither of them had any control, the more she felt compelled to make an overture to him. But she couldn't plan her approach, she told me—she would have to dive right in and blurt out something to him. That's what she did. She called Leonard and shocked him by telling him that she had felt left out when he was born. She said she had been so threatened by him that she hadn't really wanted to get to know him or like him. But now that she understood more about her feelings in childhood, she wanted to see if things could be different between them.

Leonard had always wanted to be friends with Norma, but he had given up after years of trying. He was a bit suspicious when she called, but was soon won over by the idea that he might have a sister after all.

They talked about their shared but separate experiences in the family. They agreed that their relationship was valuable to them and decided to work on it. They were determined to get to know each other, even though both of them initially described their relationship as "hopeless" and "horrible."

Although Norma had felt no driving need to make amends with Leonard—in fact, when she came to see me that was the furthest thing from her mind—the problems she was having out in the world motivated her to resolve their relationship. To do so, she had to be open to seeing the part she played in their relationship and in her problems with other people. She was willing to look closely at her own behavior because she so desperately wanted to understand what was wrong in the present—at work, in love, and in friendship.

As she and Leonard continued to work on their relationship, Norma softened. She became less fearful of loss and abandonment. She became less defensive at work as she began to trust more people. She also found a friend in her brother. And Leonard found, finally, the sister he had always wanted.

What You Can Do

If you and your sibling fulfilled different needs for your parents, as Norma and Leonard did for their mother, your sibling relationship has probably suffered. If there was little overlap between your roles in the family, you and your sibling may have little in common and your relationship may be layered with distance, anger, resentment, confusion, or envy.

Chances are you don't realize that you're reacting to parental expectations; you're far more likely to label the problem between you and your sibling a personality conflict. As a result, you probably react strongly to other people who have personality traits similar to your sibling's. As Norma learned, these reactions often lead to problems at work or in love.

To work on a relationship, someone has to take the first step. Usually it takes one person who is working on family issues in therapy, like Norma, or who has grown in other relationships to make the overture toward an improved sibling relationship.

In therapy, Norma remembered remarks her mother had made to her about needing her and comments her mother had made to Leonard about his being her "little man." These memories helped Norma to see the different expectations her mother brought to her relationship with each child. If you can remember comments such as these, the recollection will be helpful in uncovering the differing parental expectations that forced you and your sibling apart.

You can also ask your parents outright what their expectations were when each of you was born. If they are willing and able to tell you what they felt, what they wanted, and what kind of relationship they had at the time each child was born, you'll be able to work forward from there to your relationship with your sibling today.

"This Baby Will Be the Glue That Holds My Marriage Together": Parents' Relationship Needs

It's not uncommon for one or both parents to expect that having a child will keep their marriage from falling apart. Parents often hope that a child will make them feel close or happy again, that the child will bridge the distance that has opened up between them. Sometimes one parent hopes that having a child will change the partner. This is not uncommon in families where one parent is an alcoholic, where the nondrinking partner wants to believe that a child—through an increased sense of responsibility, guilt, or love—will give the alcoholic reason to stay sober.

Parents are not the only ones who have expectations about a new arrival; siblings do, too: "If that new baby thinks we're going to be friends, forget it." "Now I'll have somebody to boss around." "Maybe we can be friends and I won't feel so scared at night." "Maybe Dad will stop hitting me and hit the new kid instead."

Often the expectations of siblings mirror parental expectations. This was the case with Sam and his mother. Sam's father always made an excuse to leave shortly after dinner and sometimes didn't return home until the next night. When Sam was eight, his mother got pregnant. She told Sam, "When your daddy sees how sweet our new baby is, he won't be able to leave us, he'll be so proud." Sam couldn't wait for the baby to be born, because if his father stayed home, his mother would be happy again.

After Linda was born, Sam thought he and his mother had got their wish. His dad did stay home after dinner. When Sam heard his dad's car coming into the driveway he would run into the baby's room, wake her up, and try to comb her hair. Every day, Sam would faithfully bring Linda to his dad. Dad would set her on his lap, smile at her, then hand her back to Sam. When she started to fuss, Sam would rush the baby out of the room. "Be quiet, be quiet," he would urge while he rocked her on the edge of the bed.

When, after a few months, his father began making the same old excuses and leaving after dinner, Sam shook his sister up and down until she started to scream. "I hate you, I hate you!" he said. "If you weren't so ugly—if you would shut up—if you were a boy—Dad would stay home and make Mom happy."

It was Linda whom I saw in therapy. When she brought her brother in for a session at my request, he remembered nothing about blaming Linda for their parents' marital troubles. Sam couldn't say why he and his sister were always at odds. "I've just never liked her," he said, puzzled.

But Linda was persistent. "I don't understand it, Sam," she said to him. "You never gave me a chance. I don't feel you know who I am at all, so how can you say you don't like me?"

Linda kept at Sam because she realized during therapy that until the two of them could straighten out their relationship, she would never have a decent relationship with a man. "I was three when my father left us for good," she said to me, "and I know I have feelings of rejection about that, but I lived with Sam every day and I felt his rejection all the time."

Fortunately, Sam heard her out and was surprised at what she had to say. He had never given the relationship much thought, he said, but he was willing to do so now. "You've made me curious," he told Linda.

They talked about their parents' divorce. "When Dad left," Sam said, "it devastated me. Not so much for me, but for Mom. She would have done anything to make him stay, including having you."

When he said that, he stopped and looked at both of us. "That's right," he said, "including having you."

Once his memory was jogged, everything started to click for Sam. He now remembered with remarkable clarity what his expectations of Linda had been before she was born and immediately after. To help trigger Sam's memory, I asked him how he felt about Linda now. "I feel angry with her a lot over small things," he said. "I don't know why."

Sam's feelings were an adult version of what he had felt 20 years ago. His anger at Linda over "small things" was the same old frustration and anger he felt at her as a child, when he discovered she was not the solution to their mother's problem with their father after all.

"I was disappointed for Mother," he said to Linda later. "She loved the old man. She said having you was going to make a difference, and I believed her. When it didn't change anything, I thought it was your fault."

Changing Your Relationship

You may have clear memories of what your expectations of your new brother or sister were. Then again, you might be asking yourself what others ask me all the time: "How can I possibly remember that far back?" If you can't, remember that actions often speak louder than words: what you did or felt *then,* you might still be doing or feeling *now.* Strong feelings are good clues to your early relationships.

If you felt overly critical, protective, or resentful of your sister, or responsible for making your brother be good, quiet, or nice, you were probably responding to your parents' expectations. If you have been tuned in to your parents' feelings and inordinately concerned about their welfare, you probably expected your sibling to fall into line in some way, to also take care of your parents.

Suggest to your sibling that you get together and talk about your family. If your brother or sister does not live close by, make an appointment by phone. Talk about your feelings not only for each other, but for your parents and their marriage as well.

If your relationship with your sibling is too distant or angry for a meeting right away, you can do similar detective work on your own. Pay attention to your reactions to your sibling, and to your sibling's reactions to you. Are they appropriate to the current situation? How long have you been reacting in this way?

"If They Think They're Having This Baby for Me, They Made a Big Mistake": When Parents' Expectations Backfire

Children have minds of their own, and when parents express their expectations too forcefully, all too often the expectations backfire. For instance, if your parents insisted that you be nice to your younger brother, you may have taken every opportunity to pinch him behind their backs. Similarly, if your parents expected your younger sister to obey you, she may have gone out of her way to be rebellious and belligerent with you.

Jill's relationship with her brother is a good example of how expectations backfire. Jill was three when her mother became pregnant. Her parents told her that she was going to have a wonderful brother or sister and that they were having the baby for her. "I remember deciding then and there that I would show them," she recalled. "If they were having this baby for me, they were making a big mistake, because as far as I was concerned this kid was going to be a pain in the butt."

Parents often are unaware of the problems they create within their children's relationships. Jill's parents had never gotten along with their own siblings, and they wanted their children's experience to be different. But for all their parents' good intentions, Jill and Brad's relationship became, in their mother's words, "the worst case of sibling rivalry from day one."

As far as Jill was concerned, her brother's appearance on the scene jeopardized the love showered on her by her doting parents. "In retrospect, I think I felt tricked by my parents," she told me. "They kept saying this baby was for me, but I knew it was for them. If it was up to me, I would have kept all their love for myself."

Out of a need to prove they were good parents, Jill's mother and father tried to force their children to get along. They never saw that Jill was threatened by the new baby and so never took steps to help her overcome her feelings of displacement. Instead, they told her how she was *supposed to feel* and pressured her to love the baby immediately. In the process, Jill learned to hate her brother. As a child she slapped him, pushed him away if he tried to play with her, and teased him unmercifully. As an adult she would cut Brad off and make sarcastic comments whenever he talked. He had given up trying to have a relationship with her long ago and avoided her as much as possible.

Jill's anger at her parents for trying to control her relationship with her brother caused her to "throw out the baby with the bath water." As Jill said to me in therapy, "My parents spent the first 25 years of Brad's life trying to convince me what a great kid he was. If they had just shut up, we might have had a chance to like each other."

Once she saw that the people who were hurt the most were not her parents, but herself and Brad, Jill decided to work on her relationship with him. Brad, after resisting briefly, also opened up to her. Today they continue to scrape away the layers of anger and distance between them and are finding it possible to be friends.

What You Can Do

One way to discover whether your parents' expectations left you feeling coerced is to listen to them talking about you and your sibling now, or to recall the ways they talked about you in the past. Statements like, "You were determined not to like your brother from day one," or, "We tried so hard to get you to like your sister," or, "We thought you would take better care of your baby brother," indicate that you were under pressure to behave a certain way toward your sibling.

Parents frequently coerce their children to act a certain way toward each other, in keeping with their notions of what a "good" or "healthy" family is like. Parents who want to do the best job they can often feel anxious about their parenting abilities. This anxiety may have led them to demand certain behaviors from you and your sibling that prevented you from expressing anger, hurt, or just plain brattiness—all of which are natural reactions for siblings at times.

If you still tense up just thinking about being close to your sibling—if you think, "I'll be damned if I'll take care of her or be nice to her or help her"—then you may still be reacting to your parents' expectations.

"I Want You to Be the Tennis Champ I Couldn't Be": Stage Parents

One of the most powerful expectations parents can have of their children is that the youngsters will fulfill the dreams the parents themselves were unable to realize. Rather than seeing their children as individuals and allowing them to develop into their own persons, such stage parents view their children as offering a second chance for *them*. Their children become objects, means to an end.

We are all familiar with the stage mother who pushes her daughter into being the star the mother never was, or the father who decides that his son will be the linebacker he couldn't be. Such stage parents know exactly what they're looking for. If you come from such a family, you can tap-dance all you want, but if it's an opera singer your parents are looking for, even the most sensational tap-dancing won't make any difference. By the time you reach adulthood, you will have either stopped tap-dancing, even if you're good at it, or embraced it to the exclusion of everything else, hoping someone will notice.

If you did exhibit the skill or trait your parents were looking for, you haven't lived a life of your own; you belonged to your parents. Chances are you don't have a healthy relationship with your siblings, either. How could you? Your siblings learned either to resent you or to ignore you, or felt relieved that the pressure was off them. You either felt too special to be bothered with them, treated them like slaves, or envied them for their freedom from the bondage you felt. As adults, you're little more than strangers.

This was true for Nolan and his sister, Cindy. Their father's dream had been to be a great tennis player. He never made it, but he was determined that one of his kids would. As soon as his three boys were old enough to lift a racket, he took them out to the tennis court and started hitting balls to them for hours at a time.

"Then along came Cindy," Nolan said. "She was truly a great player." Once Nolan's father discovered Cindy's talent, he focused all his attention on her. "We felt sorry for Cindy," Nolan recounted, "but at the same time we were so relieved to be off the hook that we pressured her, too. Every time she said she was tired or didn't want to play, we would push her even harder. I feel horrible about that now."

When Nolan first came to me for therapy, Cindy had just been admitted to a hospital at the age of 16 for nervous exhaustion. I encouraged Nolan to talk to her and offer his support. When she was feeling stronger, he told her about his guilt for going along with their father and pushing Cindy so hard.

Nolan described to me how Cindy had broken down and sobbed. "It means so much to me that you're saying this now," she had said. "I felt so alone when everyone was pushing me to play. I didn't dare stop, not even for a second."

"You had to succeed for all of us," Nolan had told her.

"Cindy was the one we sacrificed to Dad's obsession," he said to me. "We never even thought about her much, or about what she was feeling. We all fell into seeing her the way Dad did—as a machine, a thing that would do for him what he couldn't do for himself."

It was easy for Nolan and Cindy to work on their relationship because they both could pinpoint where their problems had originated. Their father's obsession had clouded the relationships between Cindy and her brothers. Once they could talk about it openly, the way was cleared for them to get to know each other. With Nolan's encouragement, Cindy was able to confront her father. She eventually gave up tennis.

"My relationship with Cindy was built on the ashes of my father's dream," Nolan said to me. "In order for us to have a relationship, we had to destroy his dream."

"Your father had an obsession, not a dream," I countered. "The dream was about himself, and it should have ended with him."

Changing Your Relationship

The only kind of sibling relationship nurtured in stage families is one that feeds the parental dream. For you and your sibling to be able to build a bridge to each other, you need to be able to recognize what that dream was and how it affected your family.

Ask yourself and your sibling how much of your behavior is still being done to please a parent. Sometimes what starts out as a parent's dream becomes the child's own. If this is the case for you, claim that dream for yourself. Don't do it for Dad or Mom. Do it for yourself.

If your sibling is the one satisfying your parents' dreams, ask him or her what it feels like. Tell your brother or sister how you felt growing up—left out, resentful, relieved. Express your concern that your parents are still dominating your relationship with your sibling.

If appropriate or necessary, as in Nolan's case, help your sibling to confront your parent. Make an alliance with your sibling. Give her whatever support she needs. Offer assurance to them that you understand and agree that your sibling doesn't have to live her life to satisfy your parents.

"We're One Big, Happy Family": The Power of Family Myths

Many families labor under the weight of a myth. If your parents insisted that yours was "one big, happy family," you probably believed them even in the face of evidence to the contrary. Living in a family where a myth was promoted meant that you and your siblings played assigned roles and were not permitted to be real with one another. If yours was a "happy" family, then happy you had to appear, both inside the family and outside it.

Because your family operated under a myth, you find it difficult to talk about your real feelings. In fact, you probably don't even know what your real feelings are—and if occasionally they break through, you deny them. Perpetuating the family myth demands that you deny any feelings counter to it. But a family's reality is often the opposite of the myth family members cling to.

This was the case in my family. We believed we were a close family and presented that picture to the world, but we weren't close in the normal definition of the word. My family was in upheaval most of the time because of my father's alcoholism and my mother's emotional volatility. Periods of fighting and shouting were followed by angry silences that would last for weeks. But even if my parents had been up all night fighting, we would show up at church the next morning, the kids clean, polite, and smiling, Dad with a hell of a hangover but charming as usual, Mom furious but smiling at everyone as if all was well.

As adults, my brother, sister, and I persisted in believing we were close. For myself and my siblings, "close" meant that when Dad drank or Mom became angry or depressed, we would band together and try to fix the problem. We never talked about ourselves, about what was happening in *our* lives.

Not until our family myth was exploded could we really be close. That happened about 20 years ago, when my father almost died from a drinking binge and was hospitalized for two months. During his stay in the hospital, our whole family attended a group therapy session. We sat uncomfortably in a large circle with five or six other families and one therapist. Joanne, Harry, and I took our place with Dad, who looked like he should have died, and Mom, who looked like she wished he had. We commenced chirping away about what a close family we were.

The therapist leaned so far out of her seat, I thought she would fall on the floor. Calmly but intensely, she told us exactly what our family was really like: the silences, the physical fights, the yelling, the months of things being "fine" followed by the months of horror. How did she know? It was as if she had been hiding under one of our beds for the last 20 years.

This single session was one of the most powerful, frightening, freeing experiences of my life. When the therapist confronted us with the truth about our family life, a curtain rose for me, and everything in my life was different from that moment on. For me and for my family there was no turning back. That day the myth we had used to sustain us went up in smoke.

Joanne, Harry, and I had no choice but to start over; the old rules no longer applied. Joanne and I immediately decided not to involve ourselves in our parents' relationship any longer. At first Harry was frightened, insisting that terrible things would happen if we didn't rescue our parents as we always had.

My parents' relationship worsened when my father came out of the hospital. He stayed sober, and partly as a result of his sobriety, my mother's emotional problems surfaced. During the next several months Joanne, Harry, and I did not intervene in our parents' struggles. Instead, we talked to one another about how frightened and helpless *we felt* as we witnessed their relationship disintegrating. In talking about our own feelings, we became closer. Finally our closeness was based on reality, not myth.

My parents eventually separated. My father returned to Alcoholics Anonymous and never took another drink. I'm still very proud of him for those last sober 18 years before he died.

What You Can Do

Family myths put constraints on siblings. If you and your brothers and sisters lived in a "perfect" home, you couldn't share your vulnerabilities. If you lived in a "cursed" family, your lives were as eventful as a soap opera, and you're probably still living the dramatic life with a flourish.

Relationships outside the family are probably difficult for you. You were taught to trust the people who maintained your family myth and to mistrust anyone who challenged it. Now that you are an adult, lovers, friends, and spouses are often a point of contention between you and your siblings. None of you feels much trust for outsiders—outsiders generally don't buy your family myth—and any of you who forms a relationship with someone outside the family is suspect. The fear of exposure or betrayal is powerful, and you may be blackballed if you seem to be getting too close to an outsider.

If you have managed to have a separate relationship, you probably maintain a life with your family of origin that does not include your spouse or lover. Harry, Joanne, and I all had outside relationships, but when anything happened in our family, we closed ranks. We didn't include our lovers or spouses in our family drama.

Sometimes it proves easier not to marry at all. Perhaps you and your siblings have ended up alone, feeling intensely loyal and protective of one another, but living in a world that cannot be shared because it's a lie. That's one of the tragedies of siblings who live with a family myth: devastating isolation. Working together to perpetuate the family myth has given you a false sense of closeness with your siblings but it is a feeling that no one else can share.

You, as an individual, must confront your family myth head-on. Once the curtain parts for you, your family will never look the same again. But be prepared for your family to fight against your newfound reality. You may be branded a traitor for challenging the myth; your brother or sister may not be able to see how to let go of the myth without the whole family collapsing. It may feel easier and safer for your sibling to sacrifice you than to listen to the truth.

It's rare for all siblings in a family to accept the truth about a family myth at the same time. I consider myself lucky because my whole family was confronted at once by someone outside the family. If you are alone in recognizing your family myth and do not want to be sacrificed, you will have to find a balance between your empathy for your siblings and your need to hold on to your reality.

Try talking gently to your brother or sister about what you've discovered. Most important, remember how you felt when you believed your myth. If your sibling gets defensive, drop the topic, but begin to be more honest about who you are and in what ways you don't fit into the family myth. For instance, if you come from a "happy" family, try mentioning an event in your life or a movie that made you feel sad. You will probably be met with silence, then a quick recovery by your sibling into "happy mode." Accept his need to go back into his comfort zone. But repeat this honest behavior in small ways every time you are together.

Over time your sibling may begin to hear you. The process will be frightening and you will both feel uncertain. This is natural. It will take time for you to adjust to being yourself with your sibling and also with other people.

"Don't Tell Anybody Outside the Family": Living with Family Secrets

Siblings also become isolated from the outside world when parents conceal such things as dad's drinking, mom's nervous breakdown, a son's epilepsy, or a grandmother's sordid past. These parents force their children to enter into the secret.

If you grew up in a family with a secret, you learned that to have problems is a shameful thing, something to be hidden, something never to be discussed, not even in your own family. As adults, you and your sibling can't share your own lives with each other because your parents taught you that airing dirty laundry is reprehensible, weak, and humiliating.

You probably have trouble knowing what's "correct" to say about relationships, how much to reveal of your life, or how much to keep private. Perhaps you go overboard in response, feeling that the only antidote to secrecy is absolute honesty, or maybe you are secretive about everything.

When I first started seeing Eric in therapy, he was having a lot of difficulty with relationships. His tendency was to be secretive, not out of deviousness but out of fear and confusion. He was involved with a woman whom he liked very much, but she had already told him she mistrusted him. "You look stricken if I ask you a simple question like what you had for dinner," she had said to him. "How can I trust you to answer the big questions like, 'Will you be faithful?'"

"I'm afraid that if I say too much about myself, it will be used against me," Eric explained to me. This fear is a logical conclusion for someone who grew up in a home with secrets. When you're told that you must keep a secret from the world, the assumption is that the world will harm your family if your secret comes out. Children feel a deep sense of shame when something so awful is going on at home that they must hide it from others they care about, such as teachers and friends. When Eric first told me about his father's drinking and compulsive gambling, he said he felt like a "worm, a slimy thing."

Eric was aghast when I suggested that he talk to his brother, Ron, about how it felt having to live with their secret all their lives. "I can't betray my parents," Eric said. "They would both be so ashamed."

"I wasn't talking about your parents, I was talking about Ron, your brother," I replied. "He already knows. Where's the betrayal?"

"Well, I know he knows, but we don't talk about my parents. It would just hurt them even more."

After many discussions with me about the issue, Eric finally called Ron and they met for dinner. Eric related, "When I mentioned I was in therapy, Ron looked petrified. I almost gave up right then."

Eric didn't give up, though. He told Ron about the tremendous sense of relief he felt when he first told a therapist the family secret. He explained that he wanted to talk to Ron about it because he realized how much that secret had interfered in their relationship. "I'm not saying we should tell the world about it, Ron," he had said. "But, between you and me at least, it has to be acknowledged. I want to talk about what it felt like having to hide Dad's problem from the world."

Ron listened, and as Eric continued to talk, Ron's reaction shifted from panic to relief. "God, Eric, I can't tell you how good your words sound to me," he said, with tears in his eyes.

They stayed at the restaurant until it closed and then walked the streets of Santa Monica for hours, talking. "It was like someone opening the floodgates for us," Eric told me. "We both had so much to say, not only about the family stuff, but everything. For the first time, I feel like Ron and I had a real conversation. We're going to meet at the same place next week."

Changing Your Relationship

The inability of siblings to talk to each other about their parents' secrets is one of the major blocks to an open relationship. It has to be surmounted if you are to achieve closeness with your sibling. Your parents' sense of shame or privacy should not take precedence.

If you come from a family with a secret, you will be terrified of this first honest conversation. But your parents will not die if you talk about their secret. They may complain, be angry, ostracize you, or make you feel guilty, but they will survive. You have a right to have a close relationship with your brother or sister. Let your parents take care of themselves. That's what they should have been doing all along.

If you're not yet comfortable with the idea of talking openly about your family secret with your sibling, you can still reach out to him and tell him you want to have a closer relationship with him. Work on being honest about your own life, and encourage him to be honest about his.

If you tend to be secretive, make a point of telling your brother or sister something you would normally keep secret, such as where you went the night before or whom you were with. If you tend to reveal everything, work on tolerating your sibling's need for privacy. Don't push him to tell you all. Your relationship needs to include a healthy respect for each other's personal boundaries.

Once you and your sibling understand that aspects of your behavior toward each other are based on expectations your parents had—expectations that were out of your control—you may find it easier to put aside your anger or jealousy and build a new relationship.

CHAPTER THREE

"I'm Not Your Little Brother Anymore!"

Equalizing Sibling Relationships

Every culture deems certain behaviors appropriate to older and younger siblings. Television, books, and movies are packed with heroic older brothers protecting younger ones. Older sisters most often make their appearance as nurturing, disapproving, or hyper-responsible. Sitcoms are full of younger siblings who either torment or entertain their older brothers and sisters.

Such stereotypes affect parents, who treat older and younger siblings differently and expect them to behave differently. "You're older—you should know better." "You're too young, listen to what your older sister says." "You have to set a good example for your brothers and sisters." "Isn't your little sister funny?" Parents typically express disappointment in their older children—"I expected more from you"—and frustration with younger children—"When are you going to grow up?"

During childhood, these cultural and parental stereotypes exert pressure on relationships between brothers and sisters. When you have to act a certain way because your parents or the culture demands it, you can't bring all of yourself into your relationships. If big brothers must always be strong, they can't ever show vulnerability; if big sisters must always nurture their younger siblings, they can never ask for nurturing themselves; if little brothers and sisters must always be cute or entertaining, they can never relax.

Likely as not, these roles have affected not only your sibling relationships but all your other relationships as well. If you are accustomed to being the supportive older sister, you probably find yourself in that role in love, work, and friendship. If you felt displaced by a younger sibling, you probably resent others for being in the spotlight. If you are the baby of the family, you probably rebel against people who remind you of your older brother, or surround yourself with friends and lovers who encourage your antics and cover for you when you make a mess. If you had older siblings who were go-getters, you may feel inadequate around aggressive people.

As a youngster, you focused on development, and your siblings served as your measuring stick; you noticed what your older siblings did that you couldn't do yet, and what you could do that your younger siblings weren't capable of. When children are young, birth order is one of the most enduring ways they identify themselves, both within and outside the family. "She's my older sister," "I'm the youngest," "He's the one in the middle," and so on. These descriptions help children place themselves in relationship to their siblings.

Now that you and your siblings are adults, birth order is no longer relevant, yet you and your siblings may continue to let small age differences dominate and define your relationship.

Birth-Order Blues

In adulthood, birth-order problems may masquerade as something else. By answering the following questions, you can determine whether you and your siblings are still locked into a relationship dominated by birth order, and whether your work or love relationships are ruled by these same patterns.

If you are an older sibling:

Do you feel that you carry the burden of every relationship?

Do you like telling your co-workers or younger siblings what to do, but have difficulty asking for help or trusting others' judgment?

Do you worry that your sibling or co-worker is hogging all the attention from you?

If you are a younger sibling:

Do you ask for or expect co-workers, your sibling, or spouse to make excuses for you?

Do you feel as if everybody is telling you what to do, just like your sister or brother did?

Do you wish people would take you seriously?

If you answered yes to any of these questions, you'll find this chapter helpful in equalizing your relationships.

Sibling Inventory

Write down all the physical and emotional characteristics you can think of to define your sibling. You should be able to write at least 25. If your sibling is willing, have him or her do the same about you. Read aloud what you have written about each other, or have someone else read it. How accurate is your perception of your sibling now?

In this chapter I'll discuss how reactive patterns and sibling myths help to maintain the power discrepancies of sibling relationships. I'll describe some problems that are typically found in most sibling relationships, and the difficulties of equalizing such relationships. The last part of the chapter will focus on how older/younger sibling roles are distorted or exaggerated in troubled families.

The ability to put yourself in your sibling's shoes is one of the best ways to begin equalizing your relationship, so I encourage you to read the whole chapter, not just the parts that apply to you.

The Inherent Power Discrepancy of Childhood Relationships

Because age confers status, birth order automatically sets up a power discrepancy in the relationship. This early imbalance is resistant to change; your older brother has always been older, your younger sister has always been younger. Without thinking, you continue to react to each other in the same way, even as adults. An acquaintance of mine, Larry, told me a story that illustrates how persistent these power discrepancies are.

Last Christmas, Larry's older sister baked him some Christmas cookies and gave them to his older brother to give to Larry. "My brother got to my house," Larry recalled, "and before he gave me the box of cookies, he opened it up, looked inside, saw one cookie in the shape of an airplane, popped it into his mouth, and then pushed the box toward me. I was instantly eight years old," he said. "Here was my older brother taking my things *as usual*. I grabbed the box and hugged it to my chest and screamed, 'Those are my cookies! Linda gave them to *me!*'"

Larry laughed, remembering the scene. "I'm sure I had the same indignant look on my face, too. My brother looked at me, smiled, and said the same thing he had always said: "Oh yeah? What are you gonna do about it?" Larry is close to 50, and his brother is approaching 60.

Reactive responses become entrenched when an older sibling moves into a new developmental stage and leaves a younger sibling behind. Siblings are commonly at a loss to cope with these sometimes sudden changes. They often revert to name-calling, angry silences, withdrawal, polarization, and other reactive responses because they don't know how else to discharge their anger, fear, jealousy, and confusion. This is what occurred between my clients Connie and Mitch when Mitch became a teenager.

"He's a Jerk," "She's Immature": Reactive Responses

To his 11-year-old sister, Connie, Mitch seemed to flip-flop from one day to the next. Suddenly all he was interested in was girls, cars, and sex. Whereas before Connie and Mitch had been close and did many things together, now he wouldn't give her the time of day. She was a "pest," a "baby."

Connie felt rejected and abandoned. In her estimation, her brother had turned into a sex-crazed maniac overnight. She searched his room until she found where he was hiding *those* magazines; she drew mustaches over all the important parts.

When I met Connie and Mitch they were both in their thirties, yet they still talked to each other as they had twenty years ago. Mitch insisted on seeing himself as the older, wiser sibling, and his attitude drove Connie crazy. "He's just a jerk, he doesn't know anything," she would say. "She's so immature," Mitch would shoot back.

It took someone from outside the family to challenge their behavior. Shortly after Mitch became engaged, he and his fiancée, Vicky, were driving home from an evening at his parents' home. Vicky told him that his constant bickering with his sister was tiresome. "You're like two irritating teenagers," she said. "And, on top of it, every single time we leave your parents we get into a fight, because you're still in an argumentative mood, so you argue with me."

Mitch was surprised, but he knew Vicky was right. The next day he called Connie and told her what Vicky had said. He added that he was mature enough to stop "carrying on like a kid," but he questioned whether Connie was capable of the same feat. Connie said, "Hey, that's not the problem. The problem is, how does somebody work on liking a jerk?"

On that note, Connie and Mitch appeared in my office, eager to have me help them. The first thing I asked them to do was to take a sibling inventory. Both wrote down all the physical and emotional characteristics they could think of to define the other. I then asked them to read their lists aloud.

Mitch described Connie as pimply, nosy, and at least four inches shorter than she really was. Connie described Mitch as unattractive, loud, and obsessed with girls. Neither description fit the person. I pointed out the discrepancies between how they saw each other and reality. When faced with the evidence, they couldn't stop laughing. Once they saw how powerful their reactive patterns had been, they began to show real curiosity about each other. In a matter of months, their bickering disappeared and they became fast friends.

What You Can Do

If you made up your mind years ago about who your sibling is, look again. You might notice that your younger sister actually takes baths now and your older brother doesn't reek of pot smoke. What was once an older brother's nasty teasing may have turned into a great sense of humor.

To really open your eyes, take a sibling inventory yourself. If possible, have your sibling participate with you. If not, ask a friend, lover, or therapist to help you compare who your sibling is now with the person you remember from your childhood. Pay attention to your feelings as you write the inventory. If your stomach knots up when you write that your sister is a nosy witch, or if you get angry writing about how stupid or selfish your brother is, your feelings are a clue that you're reacting to your sibling in old, patterned ways.

Try sweeping away these old responses and see what emerges. You may discover, for instance, that your reactive angry feelings toward your older brother are covering up hurt feelings from as far back as high school, or that you are still dismissing your younger sister as a dumb kid when she's actually quite interesting.

"My Older Brother Spit in My Face": Sibling Myths

Another way that adult siblings maintain the power discrepancies of childhood is by reiterating old stories about each other. By repeating certain stories over and over, they simplify their relationships and reduce each other to one-dimensional characters.

Older siblings' stories tend to focus on their younger siblings as pests, sweethearts, or babies of the family. Many younger siblings' stories focus on older siblings who protected or tormented them when they were younger. Retelling protection stories serves to elevate the older sibling into a hero, and relating stories of abuse serves to keep the offending sibling at a distance, even if he or she has long since changed.

Joyce held on to a myth about her older brother for years. When she was young, Jack had once pinned her down in the backyard and spit in her face over and over again. She had never forgiven him, even though he had stopped such behavior long ago. Instead she told and retold the story, effectively freezing Jack into the role of bully and herself into the role of victimized little sister. She saw herself as a potential victim in other areas of her life, trusted no one, and often suspected people at work of slighting her or talking about her behind her back. She even used her anger at her brother to keep her husband at a distance.

I suggested to Joyce that if she could understand her anger at her brother, she might gain some insight into what was happening in her life. At my urging, Joyce made an effort to get to know Jack over a period of several months. She was astonished to find how much she liked him. Eventually she was able to tell Jack that the reason she had been cold and distant with him all these years was because he had spit on her when they were kids.

He was shocked to learn how she had been affected by his actions. "Well," he said finally, "I didn't know how to be affectionate. Believe it or not, spitting on you was probably my way of trying to be close."

As they talked, Joyce and Jack realized how harsh and critical their parents had been. As a child, Joyce had hoped to find in her brother a safe haven. When he spit in her face that day, she closed down, convinced there was no love anywhere in the world. Her story about her brother, she came to see, was a metaphor for her entire family. Once Joyce regained her brother, she was able to put aside her role as a victim and to learn more rewarding ways to express her feelings.

Changing Your Relationship

Are there certain stories that you tell over and over about your brother or sister? It's important to see why you have chosen to hold on to particular stories about your sibling. My client Rachel recalled how her younger brother, Jacob, had crawled onto her lap when he was four years old and said, "I want you to be my mommy." To her, Jacob's behavior signified what a good big sister she was. A friend of mine, Dennis, recalled frequently how his older brother walked him to the park every Saturday, leading him through their dangerous neighborhood so Dennis could play baseball. This myth reinforced his feelings about his brother being his heroic protector.

Often siblings rely on such myths as a way of staying connected. Dennis and his brother, for instance, had lost touch with each other and felt they had nothing to connect them but their past. If this is the case with you and your sibling, it's likely that you, too, share myths about each other. If you attempt to connect through myth-tinged memories, you may feel a momentary glow, but relying on the old days to give you a sense of closeness keeps you buried in the past.

The bridge to the present is to find out who your sibling is now, not to stay with a remembered image. Instead of repeating a familiar old story when you want to feel close, try asking your sibling what's going on in his or her life now.

Don't forget your stories or devalue them. Your memories and perceptions of each other are priceless, one of the facets that contribute to the multilayered complexity of the sibling relationship. But don't make your myth *the relationship*.

Equalizing Sibling Relationships

The younger/older dynamic operates in all families, no matter how large. Even middle children experience the dynamic in relation to their older and younger siblings. The following section looks at each side of this issue as well as the best ways to go about equalizing a sibling relationship.

"What Is It Going to Take for You to See Me as a Grownup?": The Dilemma of the Younger Sibling

It's common for older siblings to take care of and make excuses for younger siblings well into adulthood. The price younger siblings pay for these perks is a lowered feeling of self-worth, competence, and independence. Even in adulthood, their older siblings may tease them and dismiss any advice they have to offer. Lovers, friends, or employees also may not expect the best from them.

This was clearly the case with Buddy. His family, especially his mother and older sister, Reba, spoiled him and made excuses for him. His older brother, Clark, thought Buddy was funny and otherwise dismissed him as a "goof-off." Buddy made a career of entertaining his classmates and never paid attention to what his teachers were saying. Consequently he did poorly in school.

Whenever Buddy failed, even as an adult, the family always had an excuse for why he wasn't living up to his potential. He surrounded himself with friends and girlfriends who thought he was "fun" and "a real character."

When I saw Buddy in therapy, he was in his late twenties. He sought counseling because he had fallen in love with a strong-willed, loving young woman who was pushing him to "get serious about his life." Maryanne was constantly speaking to the competent side of Buddy. "You can do better, Buddy," she would say. "You just give up too soon." Maryanne intrigued Buddy because he knew she was right, but what she said also frightened him.

With Maryanne's encouragement, Buddy went back to school with a definite plan to become a teacher. When Clark flew into town for Thanksgiving and heard the news, his response was to nod knowingly. "He's not mature enough to stick with it," Clark told Maryanne.

For the first few semesters Buddy excelled, then he began falling into his old patterns of not studying and not showing up for classes. Maryanne didn't pressure him, but she didn't laugh at his jokes about his teachers, either. She pointed out his own responsibility for passing or failing. Immediately Buddy withdrew from Maryanne and began spending more time with Reba, whom he felt was "understanding and not so demanding."

After several weeks of avoiding Maryanne, Buddy came into my office, sat down, and said, "Well, Maryanne did a real number on me. She made me see that I'm capable of more. Hanging around with my family and being a failure doesn't feel that good anymore."

From that session on, Buddy decided to take up the challenge of moving into adulthood with his siblings. This meant not only accepting the responsibilities of an adult, but getting his siblings to accept him as an adult, too. Buddy practiced talking to Clark and Reba in an adult voice. He stopped trying to entertain Clark every time they talked. When Clark was visiting, Buddy pointed out to him every instance in which the older brother did not listen to Buddy, did not respect what Buddy said, or doubted Buddy's ability to make decisions. Soon, with practice, Clark was responding to him in a more adult way. At the same time, Buddy also began pointing out to Reba his successes in the world. By reminding her of the things he did right, he was also reminding himself that he was capable and that it wasn't always someone else's fault when he screwed up.

To get to know his siblings better and to shift the focus off himself and his problems, Buddy started to ask them questions about themselves. This was a little more comfortable for Reba than for Clark, but neither sibling warmed to this new dynamic immediately. Buddy didn't push, but he did keep asking. Instead of waiting for Clark to call him, he started initiating the calls just to say hello. When Clark made critical remarks or Reba spoke in a condescending voice, Buddy calmly told each of them how their treatment made him feel.

Over time, Buddy's relationship with Clark and Reba improved. Then, one Friday night, instead of going to class, Buddy dropped by his parents' home for dinner because he knew Clark was in town and Reba would be there. When Reba asked about his class, he said he just didn't feel like going. "The class is boring and the teacher is a jerk," Buddy said.

Reba asked if he could afford to miss a class. Clark told him he was almost done and to hang in a little longer. Buddy spun around and screamed, "Give me a damn break, okay? Stop expecting so much from me, I'm doing the best I can," and stormed out.

When Buddy described his experience to me the following day, he was outraged. He felt misunderstood and certain that his family offered him no support. It was a difficult moment. I worked with Buddy to determine if he was being fair to his older siblings. Slowly Buddy saw that he wanted it both ways: Sometimes he still wanted to be an irresponsible little brother. Sometimes he wanted to be a responsible adult, a peer to his brother and sister. He realized that the evening before, they had reacted to him exactly as he said he wanted them to: as an adult.

Finally we talked about Buddy's deepest fear: "I'm afraid I'm going to fail," he said. Buddy had to confront this feeling on his own, without interference or help from anyone. Facing his fears, Buddy eventually became stronger.

He apologized to Clark and Reba the next day. His forthrightness brought the siblings even closer together and reunited them in their efforts to change their way of relating to one another.

What You Can Do

One of the best ways to shed the constraints of the younger sibling role is to practice acting like an adult, as Buddy did. If you ordinarily wait for your sibling to call you, try reaching out to her first. If you laugh when your brother teases you about being irresponsible or the baby of the family, try pointing out to him that you are an adult now. If you usually let others take the rap for you, begin taking responsibility for your own mistakes.

Most important, if you usually seek out people who see you as irresponsible, be open to meeting people who see the competent side of you instead. Learn to spot such people and welcome them into your life. Seek them out in work, friendship, and love. They will lovingly challenge you to be the best you can.

"You Never Ask About Me": The Dilemma of the Older Sibling

While younger siblings often manipulate older siblings into taking care of them, older siblings often manipulate younger ones into looking up to them. If you're an older sibling, you may enjoy the ego satisfaction this role brings, but you're probably not getting many of your own needs for support met. You might vacillate between feeling used and needed by your younger sibling. When you feel used, you're angry and resentful. When you feel needed, you feel good, helpful, and wise. This was the case with Clare and her two younger sisters, Yvette and Janet.

Clare came to see me because her physician had recommended psychotherapy. She had developed ulcers and was suffering from insomnia and nervous tension. For the last two months, her husband's sister and brother-in-law had been living with Clare and her husband while they looked for a place of their own. Clare worked full-time and then came home and cooked for the entire family. No one volunteered to help, and she never asked. To add to her burden, her sister-in-law constantly brought her problems to Clare, who listened for hours. Clare complained to me about the situation. When I suggested that she deserved to get some help, Clare waved me off and said, "I can handle it."

When I asked for some family history, Clare told me that she had two younger sisters. Yvette was eight years younger, and Janet was five years younger. Clare felt closer to Janet than to Yvette, but there was a barrier between them also. When I asked what the barrier was, she said, "They don't really know who I am, but I know who they are because I helped to raise them."

The pattern of Clare's life slowly emerged. She was the ultimate big sister to everyone; everybody came to Clare with their problems, but *she* felt all alone. During one session Clare complained that she had spent an entire evening with Yvette, and all they had discussed was Yvette. "We sat there all night, and she never shut up. It doesn't occur to her that I might be going through a tough time, or that I have problems too," Clare fumed.

"Does your sister know you feel angry at her?" I asked.

Clare looked angry. "Of course she doesn't know. I just said she doesn't pay any attention to my feelings."

"Well, I bet you're not giving her much of a signal either," I said.

Clare shrugged her shoulders and changed the subject to her husband and his sister, who, she said, were likewise egotistical and uncaring.

I felt obligated to confront Clare with the fact that she didn't want to give up the power that came with being a big sister. "You want it both ways," I said. "You want to complain about how everybody uses you, but you don't want to open up to anybody. You're playing it safe. You've got everybody's number, but nobody's got yours."

By holding back her life, by listening and asking about theirs, Clare, like other older siblings, held on to power. I suggested that to change her relationship with her sisters, Clare should begin sharing details of her life with them. The next time Yvette called, Clare began talking about herself a little. She felt exposed and uncomfortable and didn't say much. Yvette was so unaccustomed to Clare revealing anything about herself, she was shocked into silence for a brief moment; then Yvette reverted to talking about herself and didn't acknowledge Clare's feelings.

Mindful of this experience with Yvette, Clare felt doubly cautious when she visited Janet. Fortunately, Janet picked up on Clare's feelings right away, asked questions, and expressed genuine interest. Over the next few months Clare shared more of her feelings with Janet.

Clare and Janet eventually developed a wonderful, equal friendship. Clare's relationship with Yvette also improved as Clare asserted her right to talk and her right not to listen. She also learned to be more assertive about sharing parts of herself with others. And, while Clare balked the first time Janet offered her advice, before long Clare came to value her sister's opinion.

A short time later, Clare politely asked her sister-in-law and brother-in-law to step up their efforts to find a place of their own.

Changing Your Relationship

If you're allowing your younger sibling to do all the talking, you're getting something from the exchange too, despite all appearances to the contrary. Perhaps you are protecting yourself from your own feelings or deriving some comfort from the role of advice-giver and wise one. In Clare's case it was a little of both. She blamed her sisters for their selfishness, but she did not acknowledge her part in maintaining the status quo.

Unequal relationships of this sort lead to resentment and dependency, an unhealthy combination that many siblings consider normal.

When you first start talking about yourself, you'll probably feel very vulnerable. If you don't get a positive result right away, you're likely to feel intense rage or hurt. But don't give up on the first try.

The moment will inevitably come when your younger brother or sister gives *you* advice. The role reversal will be difficult for you, but grit your teeth and listen. Your younger sibling is not a child any longer. He or she has something to offer.

"We Always Leave Him Out": Sibling Alliances

If you come from a family of more than two children, you may have formed an alliance with one sibling against another, or two or more of your siblings may have formed an alliance that excluded you. Sometimes these alliances are based on shared likes and dislikes, but more often they are based on birth order. Older siblings ignore a younger one, younger siblings torment an older one.

These birth-order alliances are natural in childhood; a 12-year-old usually has more in common with an 11-year-old than with an 8-year-old. However, once siblings reach adulthood, these divisions of power based on age don't make much sense. Still, you may continue to exclude a sibling out of habit, or you may find yourself excluded from a close relationship simply because *it's always been that way*. That's not much of a reason.

As children, Jason, Staci, and Brian were typical when it came to alliances; Jason and Staci, close in age, formed an attachment that excluded the younger Brian. The older brother and sister teased Brian and played tricks on him all the time. Brian wanted their approval and was constantly trying to get them to like him, to no avail. Sometime around junior high school he gave up. Soon after, Jason and Staci began to ignore him altogether.

"It's strictly habit now," Jason said to me. "When the family gets together, Staci and I spend most of the time catching up on what's happened since we last saw each other. We're polite to Brian, but basically we just ignore him.

"I have no idea who Brian is," Jason added. "I'd like to find out, but after all we've done to him, I don't think he would want to know me. We treated him pretty badly."

Even when siblings become aware of their alliances, many find it difficult to change them. The anticipation of being hurt usually keeps the left-out sibling from reaching out, while embarrassment and shame usually keep the allied siblings from taking the first step toward reconciliation.

With my encouragement, Jason phoned Brian and they got together after work one night. Over pizza, Jason admitted to Brian that he had closed him out of his life and signed on with Staci. He asked if Brian was open to the idea of getting to know each other.

Brian stared at Jason. "Is this a joke?" he asked.

Jason reassured him that indeed he was serious, but Brian needed some convincing. After all, he had spent his childhood being the butt of his siblings' jokes.

For old alliances to be resolved, the rejected sibling needs to talk about his hurt and angry feelings. Brian's memories, physical and emotional, were vivid. Jason was ready to listen; his memories of those events were strong as well. He accepted responsibility for what had happened and apologized.

Brian told Jason that because of his experiences with his siblings, he tended to feel mistrustful of friends. He was comfortable having one good friend, he explained, but was nervous in the company of two. "I keep waiting for them to make fun of me, or go off and leave me behind, or something like that. I hate it," he told Jason.

Brian's discomfort with groups of friends is a common reaction of left-out siblings. Threesomes often make such siblings nervous because, in their experience, one of the three is going to be excluded and they assume it will be them.

As time went on, Jason and Brian discussed and worked through their past relationship. As they got to know each other in the present, they became much closer and decided they liked each other a lot.

Not surprisingly, Staci was not happy about this turn of events. When Jason reassured her that he still felt the same closeness to her, she wanted to know why he hadn't included her in the "big reunion." "It would have been the old alliance all over again," Jason explained. "I owed it to Brian to meet him separately."

Staci tried making fun of Brian to see if she could revive her alliance with Jason, but Jason wouldn't take the bait. At the next family gathering, Staci felt left out. As the three siblings sat around the table talking, she became more and more withdrawn; she had no idea what her role was in this new family dynamic.

Luckily, Brian felt secure enough to open up the whole topic of alliances, and all three siblings talked about their feelings. By the end of the weekend they were laughing about the time Jason and Staci convinced Brian to swallow a moth by promising they would take him to a movie if he did.

What You Can Do

If you have been excluded from an alliance, you don't have to wait for your brothers or sisters to recognize the problem. Give them a call and tell them your feelings about being left out. Such a call might make them open to a new relationship with you. Be prepared to get hurt, though. Not all siblings are willing to give up their alliances, no matter how vestigial the bonds are in adulthood.

Sometimes it feels good just to say how you felt all those years, without expecting anything to change in the present. If your current relationships are suffering because of those childhood alliances, talking them out with your siblings will probably be helpful for you.

If you've excluded a sibling, take a new look at the brother or sister you've been leaving out. You might enjoy your sibling's company now that you're both adults. Take the first step and call. Tell your sibling how you feel about your past relationship and express interest in finding out who you both are now. Your brother or sister may jump at the opportunity, or may need to express angry or hurt feelings about the past. In order for you to have a new relationship, you have to clear out the old. Be willing to listen.

"It's Not My Fault You Were Born First": How Troubled Families Exaggerate Birth-Order Roles

The older/younger sibling dynamic is most pronounced in dysfunctional families. When parents place excessive caretaking demands on older children because they are incapable of caring for their children themselves, older siblings are forced into a parental role long before they are ready for that task. Older siblings in these instances rarely experience the pleasures of childhood, but instead are forced, while still children themselves, to look out for their younger siblings, to feed, clothe, and nurture them.

As adults, these older siblings find it hard to make the necessary shift to allow their younger siblings to be adults, too. The older siblings often try to control their siblings' lives and behavior. The result is dependency or resentment (or both) on the part of the younger siblings.

Younger siblings often feel guilty for wanting to get out from under their older sibling's thumb. On one hand, they know how much their older sibling has done for them, and they feel grateful. On the other hand, they are smothered by the older sibling's need to continue to dominate their lives. This happened in Danny's family, and it was only with extreme perseverance that he was able to extricate himself from the hold his older brother had over him and to improve the relationship in the bargain.

Danny had difficulty being assertive and was susceptible to other people's opinions of him. He was a quiet and easily intimidated man. His parents hadn't been around much, but when they were they were critical. His older brother George had been like a father to Danny and his three other siblings; George had fixed their breakfasts, done their laundry, helped with their homework, and told them how late they could stay out at night. Danny, now in his forties, was married and had two kids of his own, yet George was still running his life.

Ever since Danny moved from Chicago and resettled with his family in California, George called twice a week without fail. "You gotta buy this stock," he would say, or, "I told you last week you gotta talk to your boss," or, "You gotta show your kids who's boss. Put the kid on the line, Uncle George will straighten him out."

In therapy Danny was learning to stand up for himself at work and in his marriage. Now he began feeling the strain of his brother's dominance. The most sensible solution, we agreed, was for Danny to tell George how he felt about their relationship.

Danny tried, but what he got back was a tirade from George. All the anger George had suppressed for having to take care of Danny and the other kids for so long came bursting forth. The bottom line, according to George, was that Danny and the others owed him something now. If nothing else, they owed it to him to listen to his advice.

Danny was shaken when he saw me next. George's rage had frightened him and also helped him realize why he was so fearful of anger in general. Instead of backing down, however, Danny was determined to follow through. "I have to break through this fear if I'm ever going to feel strong anywhere else in my life," Danny said.

Danny called George back a few days later and said that he appreciated all the care George had given him when he was growing up. But now he wanted a brother, not a parent. "It's not my fault you were born first," Danny said. "The anger you feel belongs to Mom and Dad, not to me."

"You're starting to sound just like that shrink you've been seeing," George responded. "People don't go around talking like that."

George continued to call at all hours and interrogate Danny about his life. Danny would say, "Thanks for asking, but you're pretty up to date about what's going on with me. What's happening with you?"

It took years for Danny's relationship with George to change. George had never had anyone listen to him or express interest in his well-being, so his ability to share feelings had atrophied. He had also been damaged by the resentment he felt as a youngster for his responsibilities. His anger, just under the surface, was enormous. The only way he knew how to relate to people was by controlling them and by keeping himself hidden. This was similar to Clare's problem, and is a common situation for older siblings.

George and Danny continued to talk to each other. One day George casually mentioned to Danny that he was "talking to a shrink about all this family shit." Eventually the child George was never allowed to be emerged. In the process, George went through gut-wrenching pain. Danny stood by his brother through his difficult times, as did their other siblings.

Changing Your Relationship

If you're an older sibling like George, you may be experiencing similar difficulties letting go of your role as older brother or sister. You may react with anger and resentment to your younger siblings' need to grow up. After all, you feel you have devoted your life to them. But the resentment you feel belongs with your parents, who abdicated their parental role. To reclaim your life, you need to relinquish control of your siblings' lives and focus on your own, which you may have neglected since childhood.

Welcome these changes, even though they frighten you, because they offer you the best chance to finally live your life and experience your own feelings.

"I Hate You for Leaving Me": When a Sibling Leaves Home

When an older sibling leaves for college, gets married, or moves to her own apartment, she may be sad at leaving her younger siblings behind, yet excited about her new life. Younger siblings may also feel sad or angry, but generally accept their elder sibling's departure as natural. In dysfunctional families, however, a sibling's leaving home is often traumatic. When siblings in such a family are close, the older child who leaves often feels both relief at getting out and guilt for leaving his younger sibling behind to handle the situation without him. The sibling who is left often feels angry, hurt, and abandoned.

Jan and her older brother, Henry, had been very close growing up. They spent a lot of time together, and although they didn't verbalize it, they depended on each other for emotional support and friendship. This bond had helped them get through even the toughest times with their alcoholic and abusive parents. When Henry got accepted to a college in Northern California, it took him three weeks to get up the nerve to tell Jan he was leaving.

"Oh, he felt awful," Jan said when she talked to me about it. "He knew I was stuck. I was only fifteen. Where could I go? I barely spoke to him in the months before he left, and I never answered any of his letters."

"What did you want him to do?" I asked.

"I wanted him to stay with me," she said.

"But to do that he would have had to give up his life."

"I don't care. He should never have left me there with them. I'll never forgive him. Never."

Jan was 24 when I had this conversation with her. Henry still lived in Berkeley. Each time Henry visited Los Angeles, he asked her to come visit him. Each time she said she was too busy.

She resisted my suggestion that she and Henry talk over what had taken place years ago. I eventually convinced her by telling her she was stuck in the past. "You don't have to make up with Henry, but you do have to move past it to get on with your life," I said.

She finally called Henry. When she told him why she was calling, it was clear that the feelings of both siblings were as fresh as if the events had happened the day before. Henry talked about his guilt at leaving and his sorrow for the loss of their close relationship. Jan talked about her anger and hurt.

"You were my big brother. If you loved me enough you would have stayed home with me," she told him. "That's all I know, and I can't make that feeling disappear. You just didn't care enough."

Then, Jan told me, Henry said quietly, "Of course. You're right. I didn't care that much. I love you, I've felt closer to you than to anyone else in my whole life. We've been through hell together, but it wasn't enough to get me to stay home and give up my chance. I guess I hoped you loved me enough to understand that I had to get away."

As with many siblings in troubled homes, Jan and Henry had counted on each other as children for the support they couldn't get from their parents. But siblings can never fully make up for what their parents fail to give. They are, after all, only children. As they talked, Jan and Henry could see that, under the circumstances, they each had done the best they could.

This conversation was a turning point in their relationship. It took months of talking, anger, and tears for them to resolve their old feelings of betrayal and hurt, but underneath was the old bond, the memories, and the desire to be connected again. For the first time in years, Jan looked forward to Henry's Thanksgiving visit. She even talked about visiting him in Berkeley.

By working on her relationship with Henry, Jan also went through a transformation in her relationship with her boyfriend. For two years he had wanted her to make a commitment and for two years she had refused. "No commitments for me," she had told him, "because they don't mean shit."

Now she came into a session and announced that she and her boyfriend had set a date for their wedding. "I've been terrified of commitments," she said. "I couldn't trust my parents, and I thought that I couldn't trust Henry either. But I *can* trust him—not to save me or rescue me, but I can trust that he loves me. It's so good to have my brother back. I missed him so much."

What You Can Do

Children who come from homes affected by alcoholism, emotional instability, or physical or emotional abuse often count on their older siblings to take care of them. Younger siblings, forgetting that their older brothers or sisters have needs of their own, may view them as parental figures who will always be there for them. Younger siblings may have unreasonable expectations of older siblings. If this was the case in your family, it's time now to put your relationship into perspective. No matter how much your older sibling may have tried, he could not possibly be a good enough "parent," because he was only a child himself. He was not equipped to give you all the love and nurturing you needed. If you were an older sibling, you also lacked the love and nurturing you needed.

Learning to be your own best parent, finding the good parent within yourself, is the key to healing these wounds. When you can parent yourself, you can then allow your relationship with your brother or sister to be what it always should have been—a close, loving sibling relationship.

Understanding and changing your birth-order relationship will open up a whole new world for you and your sibling. Each of you will have a range of behaviors that were not available to you before. For instance, you can share your concerns and joys without one of you having to be the problem and the other the solution. Equalizing a younger/older sibling relationship is not easy, but it's well worth the effort.

CHAPTER FOUR

"You're the Intelligent One, and Your Sister Is the Pretty One"

Getting Beyond Parental Labels

Just as parental expectations mold us, so do parental labels. Labels reflect assumptions about ability and character: you are "pretty," your sister is "smart." In families, we become our labels. You may be a whiz at math, but if you've been labeled the athletic one, your mathematical aptitude is ignored. If your parents labeled your sister as stupid, you may have called her stupid as well. If your parents said repeatedly that your brother was smart as a whip, you may have wondered where that left you.

As adults, you and your sibling continue to see yourselves according to these limited and sometimes destructive labels. You probably apply similar labels to other people, cutting short conflict by categorizing people. You also might have difficulty venturing to try new things. Chances are you and your sibling don't know each other fully.

The labels that do the most harm are those used repeatedly. Judy's mother labeled her and her younger sister, Lauren, as bad. "Everything we did was 'bad,'" Judy said, "from not cleaning our room well enough to having a bad attitude or not getting home on time from school. We were 'bad' girls."

When Judy got to be a teenager, "bad" took on a totally new meaning. "I got so worn down by my mother, I remember thinking, what the hell, she already thinks I'm bad, why not give her what she expects?" Judy recalled. "I went from being a nice girl to the baddest girl in my high school. I smoked dope, I had sex, I cut classes, I stayed out all night. And, as far as my mother was concerned, nothing was different."

Lauren reacted to the "bad" label in a very different way, creating friction between the sisters. Lauren tried to be good and also tried so hard to get Judy to be good that Judy began resenting her as well as their mother. It wasn't until both women were in their thirties that they were able to understand what had occurred and bridge the distance between them.

Some labels are based in reality; one sibling may well have been prettier, smarter, or more personable than the other. As children, siblings discover these inevitable differences and learn to accept them and adjust. But parents can magnify differences by labeling them. Brothers and sisters are then robbed of the experience of working these natural differences out in a healthy way. They experience problems later in life, not only with siblings but with other people as well.

For example, my client Betty was more attractive than her sister, Esther, and was labeled the pretty one. Esther, better in school, was labeled the intelligent one. As adults, the sisters sought constant reinforcement of these labels—Betty from men, Esther from her fellow academics. Betty was intimidated by "smart women" and Esther by "pretty women"—which really meant they were intimidated by each other.

Other labels may not reflect reality but can become self-fulfilling prophecies all the same. For instance, Nola was the oldest child of seven. Whenever Nola's mother got tired, she would suggest to her youngest daughter, Jean, "You look tired, why don't we take a nap?" At the same time, she would tell Nola, "You have so much energy, Nola, you never get tired."

"My mother couldn't be direct about how she was feeling," Nola said. "She needed me to help her with the kids, so she told me I had tons of energy. When she needed an excuse to rest, she told Jean that Jean was tired. With seven kids, I understand that she needed all the help she could get, but it was very confusing. To this day, I'm not comfortable taking it easy, and poor Jean can barely make it to work and back."

Getting Beyond Parental Labeling

Becoming aware of the labels your parents used to define you and your siblings is critical to improving your sibling relationships. But what's even more important is laying claim to those parts of yourself that you've squelched or left undeveloped because they didn't "belong" to you. The following exercise is designed to help you do just that:

1. Make a list of the labels your parents used to define you.

2. Make a list of the labels your parents used to define your sibling.

3. Scrutinize the *second* list closely. What traits reside in you as well as your sibling? Which traits would you like to possess that you feel are your sibling's alone?

4. We all have more freedom than we realize—certainly enough freedom to raid our sibling's list. Try on for size those traits of your sibling that interest you. If you're serious and your sibling is playful, try participating in the playfulness instead of hanging back. If

you're shy and your sibling is assertive, try speaking out more. You'll find that your repertoire of behaviors is larger than you thought. You'll also feel much closer to your sibling.

Taking a Self-Inventory

Any kind of parental labeling deprives you of the right to explore who you are. This next exercise is designed to help you rediscover yourself. Do this exercise with your sibling if possible. If not, elicit the help of someone who knows you well and whom you trust.

First, list all your physical and emotional characteristics. You should be able to think of at least 25, and probably more. When you're done, show your list to your sibling, a friend, or your therapist. The idea is not to give anyone the power to dispute who you are, but to help you to see yourself more clearly. I'll show you what I mean with an example.

A client of mine, Richard, and his sister, Sally, did this exercise together. One of the things Sally wrote about herself was that she was not athletic. When Richard read through her inventory, he pointed out that she jogged and swam.

"Well, I only do those things to keep my heart healthy," she told him. "I'm not really athletic."

"You see yourself as not athletic because Mom and Dad always labeled *me* athletic," he countered. (Richard was an all-around athlete who competed in several sports in high school and college.)

Sally looked at him in surprise. "You're right," she said confidently, and with a flourish she erased the word "not" in front of "athletic" on her Self-Inventory.

When you do the inventory, your goal is to see yourself as clearly as possible. Don't use your sibling as a measuring stick. If you're fortunate, as Sally was, your sibling will be able to help you.

Lopsided Labels

Parents sometimes forget how hungry children are to discover who they are. Children take in what their parents say about them and about their brothers and sisters. Parents may notice certain traits in their children and comment on those traits repeatedly. A child, hearing how lively or smart or attractive a sibling is, will fill in the blanks of such lopsided labeling and assume that he or she must not be lively, smart, or attractive enough.

In the extreme, lopsided parental labeling may cause a child to create an entire identity in opposition to a brother or sister. For instance, if your sister was labeled weak and sickly, you may have become a health fanatic who has never been sick a day in your life. If your brother was labeled a big baby, you may have become so tough that you don't allow any childlike feelings to emerge and you despise people who do. In these instances your very self becomes inextricably connected to your sibling. Although you may seem to be pushing away, your sibling is nevertheless necessary to your identity: who you are is based entirely on being the opposite of your sibling.

These relationships are often hostile and antagonistic, based as they are on rejecting particular traits. As an adult, you still react negatively to your sibling and other people who share similar traits. If you and your sibling are not on speaking terms, you're probably involved in a destructive, angry relationship with someone just like him. Since you've defined your identity in opposition to your sibling, you need him or someone like him around in order to experience yourself. This is what occurred between Andrea and her brother, Carl.

"Carl Is Good at Everything": How Siblings Fill in the Blanks

Many parents cannot separate themselves from their children and instead take a narcissistic interest in their children's accomplishments. To

63

such parents, a child's successes mirror their own self-worth. If this was the case with your parents, they probably reacted with undisguised pride if you or your sibling exhibited special abilities. To their minds, your excellence reflected their competence, their parenting skills, and their good genes.

Other parents are simply awed by a child who shows special abilities. Instead of claiming ownership and responsibility, they step back and gaze up at that child, wondering how they managed to create such a supernatural being. In either case, these parental responses to special children often leave the other children in the family feeling angry or envious. This is what happened in Andrea's family.

Neither of Andrea's parents had done well in athletics or academics, so their son, Carl, who excelled at both, was something of a beautiful mystery to them. Andrea's parents labeled him a superachiever.

"They didn't *favor* him," Andrea said to me. "They *idolized* him."

Every time Andrea, who was two years older than Carl, would ask her parents for help, they would suggest she "ask Carl, he'll know how to do it." She grew to hate her brother and all the things he did so perfectly. Not surprisingly, she stopped asking for help from anyone. She rejected any efforts on Carl's part to have a relationship and began putting down him and his friends.

Andrea's reaction to her parents' adulation of her brother was to despise Carl and superachievers of any sort, and to identify herself as the opposite of a superachiever: a screw-up. She hung out with the rebels in school, did poorly in her classes, and dropped out before graduating from high school. Because she couldn't stand being around people who were better at anything than she was, she surrounded herself with people who weren't a challenge for her. Eventually she began to resent them and blame them for her boredom.

Once we delved into Andrea's background, she saw clearly that she had formed her identity based on her brother's. Once she saw the pattern of her behavior and how it originated, she worked hard to overcome her feelings of inadequacy and anger. "I guess early on I had this feeling of hopelessness," she reflected. "I think by being Carl's opposite,

I was trying to be noticed for something that Carl hadn't been noticed for first, but the only thing he didn't do first was fail. Now, that's not too clever, is it? What was the reward in that?"

The most important step for Andrea was to find out who she was aside from Carl. She had no idea what she wanted to do or what she could do. Although it wasn't easy for her to do so, slowly she began allowing people into her life who excelled at certain things. She kept telling herself that having such people in her life was a gift. She also began to challenge herself. Before, by surrounding herself with people who didn't challenge her, she never had to confront her own fears of failure and worthlessness. But neither did she have a chance to discover how good she could be. She returned to school and found she had a real interest in computers and was good at programming.

Whereas before Andrea would have struggled by herself to find solutions to problems, she now asked for help with her computer questions. The assistance she sought enabled her to move more quickly to the next level of expertise. And, when she asked a question, she was able to thank the person who helped her, a giant step for her.

"For the first time," she said, "I'm finding out how far I can go, how good I can be. Before I focused on being as bad I could be." Even her relationship with her brother improved, because she was focusing on herself, not on what he could do better than she.

She also began to see that life hadn't been easy for Carl either. He was under a lot of pressure to continue to be the genius his parents knew him to be. Because his parents looked at him as something more than human, they were a little cowed in his presence. The resulting gulf was difficult to bridge. Carl was also uncomfortable around Andrea and constantly downplayed his achievements.

After several years of therapy, Andrea was finally able to talk to Carl about her feelings. He listened and seemed to understand. He also talked about what his parents' labeling had meant to him and how hurt he had been by Andrea's constant rejection of him.

"It's going to take time for me to heal my relationship with Carl," Andrea said to me after that conversation. "We know it wasn't our fault, but we both harbor angry and hurt feelings toward each other. And I know I'm not ready to accept his feelings. But I will, someday."

What You Can Do

If you are the sibling of a superachiever, the only way your relationship with the sibling will improve is by your learning to accept and appreciate yourself. Being inner-directed is the key to your feelings of success not only with your sibling, but with everyone else in your life.

Focus on your own abilities, pay attention to what you like, and pat yourself on the back for a job well done. Do not compare yourself with anyone. Use your own achievements as your measuring stick. If you have avoided trying certain things because your sibling excelled at them, try them on for size, now.

If you and your sibling are polar opposites, work on accepting behaviors in yourself that are like your sibling's, and watch for your extreme reactions to people who remind you of your sibling. Understanding the dynamics of your response to your sibling will help you to see how polarized you have become within yourself. As long as you continue to define yourself based on who your sibling is, you are denying yourself the chance to grow.

If you are a superachiever, you may have felt either sorry for your siblings or superior to them. You may experience guilt feelings about your own abilities. Remember that it is not your fault if your sibling feels angry, envious, or insecure. Don't apologize for your specialif gts, but be aware that your having them makes life a little harder for your brother or sister.

Positive Labels

In some families each child is assigned an area of expertise; one child may be the pretty one, another the athlete, another the brain, still another the musician, and so on. When parents label their children in this way, the unspoken understanding is that each sibling will stay out of the others' territory.

Some parents hope to short-circuit sibling rivalry by giving each child a separate domain in which to excel. Others believe they are positively reinforcing their children's talents by labeling them in this manner.

As an adult from one of these families, you may be afraid to explore anything outside your own realm. You fear humiliation if you cross over into an area that has been clearly defined as "not you." If you do have interests or abilities that cross over into your sibling's domain, you may be afraid of angering or humiliating your brother or sister by exhibiting those abilities.

"My Sister Is the Artist in the Family": How Labels Prevent Siblings from Getting to Know One Another

Lena's parents were terrified of sibling competition. To prevent their three girls from competing with one another, they labeled Lena "brilliant," Marissa "beautiful," and Alice "artistic."

The sisters were sensitive and careful never to tread on one another's path. As adults, they chose men who valued them for the things their parents valued in them. Lena married another scholar, Marissa was involved with a man obsessed with her sultriness, and Alice married a starving artist like herself. The three women apparently had virtually nothing in common.

When Lena entered therapy, she was troubled by the distance she felt between herself and others. She and her husband were caught up in the academic life: presenting papers at conferences, getting their research published, keeping up with the literature in their fields. Until recently, she told me, she felt there was little time for anything else. "But other people make time for families and friends," she said, "so I must be avoiding it."

I questioned her about her family history. She described her parents, then mentioned briefly that she felt the same distance between herself and her sisters that she felt with others. She wanted more closeness, she said, but didn't know how to get it. When I asked what was missing, she couldn't say. "I don't understand," she said. "We already do all the things sisters are supposed to do with each other, but we're oddly disconnected."

What we discovered was that Lena's notion of the "things sisters are supposed to do with each other"—being pleasant but staying out of each other's way—was precisely what kept them disconnected. Eventually she saw how her parents had molded the three sisters into their roles and how each of them had backed off from the others.

The current situation was complicated by the fact that Lena had always been interested in fine art and had recently taken some painting classes. When she was with her siblings or parents, however, she never mentioned her painting because she "didn't want to hurt Alice's feelings."

"Why would it hurt Alice's feelings?" I asked.

"Well," she said, "she's the artist in the family. I don't want to invade her territory."

Over time, Lena realized there was another reason she was reluctant to reveal her interest in painting to her sister: she was afraid of making a fool of herself by venturing out of her territory. Lena feared failure, and because of her need to protect her sister, she also feared success!

Once Lena understood what had gone awry in her family, she began working on expanding her relationships with her sisters. One of the first steps she took was to tell Alice about her painting. Alice didn't crumble, nor did she get enraged. Instead she hugged Lena and told her she couldn't wait to see her work. Relieved, Lena blurted out how afraid she had been of telling Alice about her painting and why. At first Alice looked surprised, then she nodded and said she had experienced similar feelings. "There was always some invisible barrier between us," Alice told her. "I never understood why, but what you're saying strikes a familiar chord."

Marissa was the one who had been hurt the most by their parents' labeling. Because her parents focused on her physical attributes, her development of self was shallow, and she suffered from both vanity and insecurity. She needed constant reassurance, yet even when she received it she felt empty inside. Her sisters, on the other hand, had each developed an inner life and meaningful work. Marissa went into therapy to discover and nurture a deeper sense of herself and her value as a person. Meanwhile, her sisters were supportive and encouraged her whenever she showed interest in things other than her physical self.

By discovering the limitations of the labels their parents had imposed on them, all three sisters were able to expand their definitions of themselves and to have a fuller, more honest relationship.

Changing Your Relationship

Doing the exercises at the beginning of this chapter (listing parental labels and taking a self-inventory) is a good place to start. Encourage your siblings to be more adventuresome in trying on new behaviors, even those that trod on "your" territory. This, of course, requires that you work through your own fears about them competing with you. If you were the "pretty" one, compliment your sister when she looks nice. If you were the "intelligent" one, comment when your brother says something interesting.

If your brother or sister appears threatened by your explorations, talk about your feelings. Be supportive and encourage your sibling to discuss how the labeling in your family put all of you into little boxes.

Of course, this is a delicate subject if your sibling is insecure about her territory. But you cannot continue to tiptoe around that insecurity, because it is a problem your sibling must come to face on her own.

Negative Labels

Often parents dismiss kids with a quick phrase—"She's a slob," "He's insensitive to his little sister," "She's mean," "He's selfish." By negatively branding their children in this way, parents teach them to fling labels at one another whenever they have conflicts.

Negative labels encourage anger and reactive responses. If you came from a family like this, as an adult you probably resort to name-calling as a way to handle differences between yourself and others.

Negative labeling severely damages a child's self-esteem. Children labeled this way grow up to be extraordinarily sensitive to criticism, either rejecting helpful comments from supervisors or friends or taking in every bit of criticism they hear, whether it is accurate or not.

I once worked with a client who had been labeled so negatively by her parents that she came into a session one day devastated because a stranger on the street had said, "Put some lipstick on that face." She took his comment as much to heart as she would a serious criticism of her work from the president of her company. All criticism held the same power to devastate her.

"You're a Slob/a Flake/a Loser": How Labeling Prevents Siblings from Working Out Their Problems

If you grew up in an atmosphere of negative labeling, you may not have much of a repertoire for problem-solving. If your brother screamed "Selfish bitch!" every time he was displeased with you, no matter what the issue was—and you screamed back "Pond scum!"—chances are your joint reasoning abilities came to an abrupt halt. This was the case with my client Anna and her sister, Sara. Their readiness to label each other and other people in their lives prevented them from working through even the most basic problems.

At the root of their problem was the fact that their parents didn't know how to have a productive argument. Whenever they were angry they would call each other names. They also labeled their daughters' behavior at the least provocation. Rather than learning how to work through their differences by compromise and negotiation, Sara and Anna adopted their parents' labels. "You're a slob," Anna would scream when she came home from school and found Sara lying on the bed reading a teen magazine, her books strewn across their bedroom floor. "You're a robot," Sara would respond, rolling her eyes at Anna's obsessive concern for order.

As an adult, Anna was always on time for family functions, never lost her keys, and never forgot any present she was supposed to buy. Sara, on the other hand, constantly lost her jacket, arrived late, and forgot to bring whatever she was supposed to bring.

Anna's pattern in therapy sessions was to complain about Sara and her latest transgression for the first five minutes of the session, and then to pull out a list of topics she wanted to talk about and move on. When I urged her to discuss her relationship with Sara, Anna became annoyed. "I have a lot of other things I need to work on. She's a slob, a flake, and a loser. I don't want to give her any more of my time."

But the problems Anna had with her sister were the same problems she had with other people in her life. "You label everyone the same way you label Sara," I told her. "Doing that allows you to dismiss them, but nothing ever gets worked out."

Anna glanced at her list. When she saw she had planned to discuss her "sloppy" secretary, her "argumentative" boss, and her "flaky" landlady, she knew I was right.

"Doesn't everybody do that?" she asked, taken aback. "How else do you relate to people if you don't put a label on them? That's how you know who they are."

"This is how you and your sister have learned to cope with conflict," I said. "Once you label the person you're having trouble with, you never go beyond that. But you need to work out your differences with people in a constructive way, something you've never been taught."

Anna began to see how her parents had resolved things by labeling or name-calling. In the process Anna became more interested in discussing the problem with Sara. Sara agreed to come to my office the following week. Anna arrived on time and sat fuming while we waited for Sara, who arrived 10 minutes late.

"See what I mean?" Anna asked me pointedly, and then she turned to Sara. "You show up late and make me wait for you on purpose, just to be in control," she said.

Sara, who had just sat down, threw up her hands in despair. "But you've always been in control of everything," she wailed. "Things always had to be done your way."

"Oh? You don't have any control over whether you arrive somewhere on time or not?"

"Why am I always wrong? You're the compulsive one."

"I'd rather be compulsive than flaky any day."

Within less than a minute they had managed to show me exactly how they operated. Each saw the other as being in control of the relationship. Instead of staying with the issue, however, they quickly reverted to calling each other names.

Both Anna and Sara had to learn to say how they felt, not through labels, but by stating their real feelings. They practiced listening to each other without commenting or defending themselves. They also agreed to stop labeling each other, so that they would be forced to go deeper into themselves to discover what was going on.

They still fight about being in control; it's a part of their relationship. But the resentment and frustration are gone because they've learned to compromise and negotiate. One of the side benefits of their breaking through the old patterns is that Sara has become more punctual and less forgetful and Anna more forgiving and relaxed. Because they can now confront their control issues directly, the sisters no longer have any need to act out their feelings in controlling ways that irritate each other.

What You Can Do

Ask your sibling to agree that you will stop calling each other names. If she won't agree, make the vow yourself. When you're getting ready to yell "Stupid idiot" again at your sister, pause and ask yourself what you are really angry about and try to talk about that instead. Do you wish your sister would listen to you more? Would you like her to ask your opinion before she goes ahead and makes plans for your parents' anniversary celebration? Bring the real issue up with her instead of retreating behind a label.

Notice and comment when your sibling does something you like or if he is clearly attempting to change an annoying behavior.

Negative labeling is learned behavior, and it usually includes labeling yourself negatively as well. While you're trying to be kinder to your sibling and co-workers, avail yourself of the same kindness. Try to turn off that inner voice that criticizes or labels your own behavior. If you miss a turn on the freeway or forget to mail a letter, don't scream at yourself that you're stupid. Accept that everyone, even you, makes mistakes.

"Poor Curtis, He's Not Healthy Like You Are": When One Sibling Has Special Handicaps

Sometimes parents label their children as a way of trying to control them. For instance, your parents may have said you were smarter than your brother as a way to encourage you to help him with his homework. Or they may have told you your sister was being immature as a way to encourage you to act grown up.

Often this kind of control is at work when parents label one child "sick" and the other "well." Parents commonly use guilt to control the well child's reaction to the dependent or sick sibling. The parents may feel guilty themselves for being able to lead a normal life, and they project this guilt onto their well children. Sometimes parents' own dependency needs are so great that they create a sick or phobic child to keep them company at home. In such cases it's not uncommon for the parent to co-opt the healthy child as well, so that the family can "stay together."

When you're encouraged to feel sorry for a brother or sister, you develop a distorted relationship. Instead of learning to treat your sibling as an equal and to accept him on his own terms, you learn to treat him as special. This treatment is likely to exacerbate your sibling's feelings of helplessness and inadequacy and to make him angry and resentful. It's likely to make you feel guilty that you are okay, resentful when you are forced to push your own feelings aside, and fearful that something bad will happen to you, too.

As an adult you may have either turned your back on your sibling or become trapped into taking care of her. Usually the "sick" or "special" sibling does not see herself as capable. She may feel she needs your help, but she resents you for it. If you're the sick one and have been trained to be dependent and expect help, you probably resent your well sibling's good health and fortune. My client Michael's brother, Curtis, handicapped since birth, was trained in this fashion, and their sibling relationship suffered as a result. Michael's insistence on working through their problems forged a closer bond between the brothers.

Curtis was born deaf and also had some other physical and mental liabilities. Michael was born four years later, and from the time he was old enough to walk he was made to feel the burden of having a handicapped brother.

When Michael was very young, the two boys played together all the time. Then Michael went off to school and began to make other friends. He also grew tall, while Curtis never stood more than four feet. It must have been a mystery to both of them as they grew apart, the younger child overtaking the older one, who was destined to remain a child forever.

Michael's father constantly berated him for living a normal life. "How do you think Curtis feels when you go off to the movies with your friends?" he would say. If Curtis broke into an irrational rage, as he often did, and hit Michael, their father always blamed Michael. "Can't you see he's feeling bad because he can't play basketball like you can?"

Years later Michael talked with me about the rage he felt at his brother for being handicapped, for making his life miserable, and for embarrassing him. Michael also talked about the anger he felt at his father for the demands he placed on him to take care of Curtis. "I knew I was supposed to love Curtis, but I hated him for years. He hit me or bit my fingers; I would pinch him so hard he would scream, but it would be this awful scream with no sound. I felt guilty for hating him, but I couldn't help it."

Curtis realized early on what power he had over his father and relished getting Michael into trouble. "Looking back, he must have hated me for leaving him," Michael said. "We were such great friends, but then I got bigger and bigger until finally I didn't want anything to do with him."

Under the circumstances, Michael did the best thing he could do for himself: he got angry, rebelled, and left home as soon as he could. The longer Michael stayed away, however, the more he remembered the Curtis of his childhood. He believed that if his parents had handled the situation differently, Curtis might never have abused what little power he had and the brothers could have remained friends.

Armed with the knowledge that his father's manipulation had distorted his relationship with his brother, Michael decided to try to rectify the situation. Over a period of a few months he made several visits to his parents' home to spend time with Curtis. His parents were mystified, and Curtis was confused and mistrustful. Curtis started in on his old tricks—kicking Michael, taunting him, pulling his hair. Each time, Michael grabbed his hands and held them until Curtis stopped, then signed to him, "You and I are friends." Curtis would sign back "No." Michael would smile and nod yes.

One day Michael dragged out the old home videos and spent hours watching them with Curtis. Curtis pulled on Michael's shirt and then pointed at the two of them on the screen playing in the backyard. Both about the same size, they were having a whale of a good time. Both he and Curtis laughed, then Curtis turned to Michael and made the sign for "Brother." Michael nodded yes and signed back "Love."

Now, Michael's eyes fill with tears whenever he talks about Curtis. They are not tears of sadness but of joy. "I'm happy because I have my brother back," he told me.

Changing Your Relationship

Avoiding the minefields of anger, resentment, jealousy, and guilt is extremely difficult in any relationship between a well sibling and a disabled sibling. If your disabled sibling cannot accept that you are well, your relationship will be filled with resentment, guilt, and envy. If you are disabled and your well sibling cannot respect and appreciate what you can do, your relationship will be filled with anger, pity, and resentment on both sides.

Don't offer your disabled sibling help unless he asks. Talk about this ahead of time. Explain that you want to respect your sibling's abilities, yet help if he needs you.

If you haven't already, ask your disabled sibling to share his experience with you. Learn about the disability so you can understand your sibling better. For example, you could walk around blindfolded for a day to experience blindness, or maneuver in your sibling's wheelchair for a day, or communicate solely in sign language for a day.

If you are disabled, learning to do as much as you can for yourself will help not only your sibling relationship, but your feelings of self-worth and self-confidence in the world. Ask your sibling to share her world with you. Talking about your frustrations without the element of blame or envy can bring you and your sibling closer instead of creating a wedge between you.

Talking about the problems between the two of you in an open, loving atmosphere is the best step you can take to healing your relationship. This is a difficult relationship on both ends, but it also presents an opportunity to forge a profound and gratifying closeness for both of you if you are willing to try.

Family Labels

Parents love to look for familial traits in their children. "Look at that nose—he looks just like Grandma Jones," they might coo at a newborn baby. It's also common for them to assign personality traits to a certain side of the family. When she skipped a grade, Cindy's parents said fondly, "She's got the Allen brains." When Charles stubbornly refused to go to bed, his mother would sigh and say, "He's got the Arnolds' stubborn streak." When these comments are innocent or represent an expression of family affection, they are comforting to children because they contribute to their sense of belonging.

Sometimes, however, this kind of labeling reflects parental competition: "My side of the family is better than yours." Sometimes it's a backhanded way to complain about a spouse. If your mother repeated all the time that your father's family was cold, you can be sure she found your father cold, too.

When parents begin to fling familial labels around, children often get caught in the crossfire. For example, whenever my sister, brother, or I would dare deviate from the straight and narrow, my mother and her family would say we were "just like the McDermotts." This meant we were headed straight into a life of drunkenness and hedonism which sounded scary at age 7, but started sounding pretty good around age 14 or so. My father, on the other hand, would sometimes react to judgmental, uptight people by joking with his brother about their being "just like the Colavecchios."

In the worst case, parents use familial labels to take ownership of a child (or children) and cede ownership of the other child (or children) to the spouse. This leads to competition, distrust, and distance between siblings. If you grew up in such a family, you and your sibling were left to fight your parents' battles and had little time to get to know each other.

"You're a Brewster and Your Sister Is a Piccone": When Siblings Are Divided by Family Labels

My client Brenda and her sister, Elaine, were stuck in this kind of bind. Brenda's father's family was a big, noisy, working-class group, while her mother's family was wealthy and terribly proper. Although initially Brenda's parents had been attracted to each other because of their differences, they soon found themselves each defending the point of view of their family of origin.

77

When Brenda was born, relatives said she looked more like her father, and from that moment on she was told that she was "a Piccone through and through." When Elaine was born a few years later, she was dubbed a "a dyed-in-the-wool Brewster"—in other words, a member in good standing of her mother's side of the family.

For three or four years after Elaine was born, the family split holidays, going to the Brewsters for Christmas Eve and the Piccones for Christmas Day. But as Brenda's parents grew further apart, the two went their separate ways and each took a child along. From that point on, the two girls were separated every holiday. Brenda would play bocci, eat manicotti, drink homemade wine mixed with 7-Up, and sing Italian songs with her father's family. Elaine would play with her mother's doll collection, sing Christmas carols, eat roast turkey in a formal dining room, and answer questions from her aunts and uncles about her schooling.

"I can remember when we were really little, Elaine and I couldn't wait to tell each other about our holidays," Brenda noted. "But we stopped after a while. I think we were both embarrassed because our experiences were so different. Later, we made nasty remarks about each other's side of the family."

Brenda's parents molded each girl into an extreme version of one side of the family. In this way, the parents competed with each other, each trying to prove that his or her way was the best.

Brenda and Elaine became more and more distant over the years. "It was like we were strangers," Brenda said. They went to different schools, liked different foods, read different books, and spent time with different people. "I called Elaine an uptight prig once, and she responded by calling me a peasant," Brenda recalled. After both left for college, they rarely saw each other.

Things would have stayed that way, except Brenda fell in love with "a Brewster type." Her father was incensed and reacted the same way his parents had 30 years earlier. Her mother was delighted and began making overtures to Brenda. "It was like she was telling my father that she had won," Brenda said.

Suddenly her whole family drama came into focus for Brenda. "I saw clearly that I had been caught in a battle between my parents. And that made me afraid, because I realized I had no idea who I was. I had believed I was a Piccone and that any part of me like my mother had been snuffed out. But then why was I attracted to Ken, who was just like my mother's side of the family?"

Brenda contacted her sister, who was living in Connecticut. They hadn't spoken for years. Brenda laid everything out on the table: how she saw her parents' relationship and what she thought had happened to her and Elaine as a result. "I feel that any part of me that's a Brewster was allotted to you," she told her sister, "and that all the Piccone traits reside in me, which is ridiculous."

"The first thing Elaine said to me was, 'Don't speak so loudly,'" Brenda reported to me later. "I almost hung up the phone right there." Instead, Brenda said, "Yes, the Piccone side of the family is louder than the Brewsters; I've learned to be loud. But I want you to listen to what I'm saying, not to the tone of my voice."

Over the next several months the two sisters talked on the telephone, haltingly and defensively at first, but they kept at it. They finally met again when Brenda married Ken.

At the reception, Brenda ended up teaching her new husband and Elaine how to dance the tarantella, while their mother and Elaine's husband looked on disapprovingly. Elaine was mortified and embarrassed, but she kept dancing anyway.

Over the next few years both Elaine and Brenda reclaimed parts of themselves that had been denied or closed off. In the process, they discovered their old friendship and the closeness they had shared before their parents' differences got in the way.

What You Can Do

If you've been labeled as representing one side of the family, it's time for you to examine how much of yourself you've had to shut off in order to fit into that neat little package. You inherited physical and personality traits from both your parents' families. If you've been told otherwise, don't believe it. Try on some of the other familial traits for size, and encourage your sibling to do so, too.

Growing up with labels, positive, negative, or otherwise, is not only harmful to your sibling relationship, but harmful to your own burgeoning sense of self. By pushing aside the labels you lived with as children, you and your siblings can experience the joy of discovering who you really are.

CHAPTER FIVE

"Mom Always Liked You Best"

Overcoming the Legacy of Favoritism

If your parents' love was given to their children unequally, that inequality permeated your feelings about yourself. It may, to this day, dominate your relationships with your siblings. Parental favoritism surfaces in sibling relationships in the forms of competitiveness, insensitivity, anger, rage, guilt, insecurity, and envy.

Favored children often receive more goodies from their parents than their overshadowed siblings—more love and approval, more clothes, cars, or money, more hugs and affection. For the sibling who is not favored, the absence of all those things, and the desire for them, dominates his or her emotional life. Sibling relationships are poisoned by parents who label one child their favorite; favoritism makes the parent-child relationship the only one that counts. For instance, Amy was her mother's favorite. Her mother took her everywhere, showered her with presents, and would say things like, "I've always been partial to little girls," or "Amy is just like I was when I was her age." Amy's two broth-ers were entirely left out in the cold. For Amy, her mother's attention was more important than anything else; her brothers just didn't count.

Favoritism often occurs between one parent and one child, and fre-quently occurs between a grandparent and grandchild. People who would never dream of favoring one of their own children are un-abashed at having a favorite grandchild. Not only does a grandparent's favoritism wreak havoc on sibling relationships, it usually is a point of contention between the parent and grandparent as well.

A friend of mine wrote to me about her favored position with her grandmother. "I've always been my grandmother's favorite," she wrote, "and the older I get, the more I see how agreeing to be her favorite was like making a pact with the devil! It prevented me from being my *mother's* daughter and also forced me to cater to my grandmother's need to be special herself. *Very* tricky! Being someone's favorite is defi-nitely a mixed bag."

This mixed bag brings up another issue. It will become apparent in this chapter that favoritism is not always positive for the favored child. For instance, Barbara's mother favored her brother, Edgar. She protected him, fussed over him, and did things for him that he should have been doing for himself—paying his bills, fixing his dinner, doing his laundry. Barbara was left to fend for herself, and in the process became strong and independent. Edgar, on the other hand, was dependent and needy. He doubted his own abilities and believed he would be helpless with-out his mother. Whenever he got into a relationship with a woman, he was disappointed that she didn't want to take care of him like his mother did, so he always ended up back with his mother.

Parents often seem to have clear-cut reasons why they favor one child. Your father may have been convinced that your brother was more handsome, smarter, or more athletic than you. Your mother may have adored you because she thought you looked just like her. But often there is no rational, or even understandable, reason why parents favor one child over another. We've all seen parents who favor a child they think is special when it's clear that another child in the family has more special abilities. That's because favoritism is not about real specialness, it is about *perceived* specialness or, in many cases, *invented* specialness.

Playing favorites has to do not with the siblings, but with the parents' unmet needs for affiliation, alliance, loyalty, or narcissistic gratification. For example, Derek's parents needed a child who would massage their own narcissism, and they decided that Derek was the one most like them. They commenced to see him as perfect—like them, of course. Derek was wonderful, gorgeous, brilliant, witty. His parents bragged about his accomplishments, noted his good looks, and dismissed his failures or struggles. His brother and sister were always second best, because they weren't the perfect specimen that Derek was, and therefore didn't reflect back the image their parents needed to believe in.

The reverse happened in Stan's family. Stan's father had been the sibling of a favored child, and he went out of his way to pay attention to the kid most like himself, the "runt of the litter," as he put it. Stan's brother, Tony, was the designated runt. Their father was always imagining slights to Tony and accusing Stan of being unfair or of trying to hog all the attention for himself. Stan's father projected his own needs on both of his children: he gave Tony the feeling of specialness he never had in his own childhood, and he said the things to Stan that he had always been afraid to say to his own brother. In this way, Stan's father relived his own childhood, but this time, he won.

My friend Heidi once asked her father why her grandmother didn't like her and liked her sister, Greta, so much. He shrugged and said, "She just does." After that simple reply, Heidi stopped looking for reasons, which was the healthiest thing she could do.

If you are busy trying to find out what makes your brother so special to your parents, you are also busy looking for reasons why you are not special. If you are the favored one and you aren't sure why, wondering about it will leave you unsure of what exactly your gifts are, particularly if what your parents value so highly in you is not what you value in yourself.

Whether you are the favored one or the sibling of a favored one, stop looking for reasons. If you think you know the reason for the favoritism, fine. Otherwise, move away from the why of it. It's painful and ultimately unproductive for the nonfavored sibling to wonder what he's missing, and it's just as unhealthy for the favored sibling to dwell on what his parents find special about him.

It's difficult for most siblings to talk openly about favoritism, unless it's done in the context of an angry "Mom always liked you best" fight. Favoritism creates a one-up, one-down feeling between siblings that makes trust almost impossible.

Favoritism is often toxic to the sibling relationship. But the legacy of a parent's favoritism can be successfully put to rest, and I've written about a number of those relationships in this chapter. I hope reading about them is helpful to you as you try to forge a new relationship with your own sibling.

Remember that favoritism is your parents' problem visited on you and your brother or sister. Sometimes that problem is so deeply ingrained that you will not be able to work it out. I've discussed a few such examples here. Fortunately, as you'll see below, you can still grow from the experience of working the situation through for yourself.

Following are some questions to ask yourself regarding your status in your family.

If you are a favored child:

Do you feel like you have done something to deserve the special treatment you receive from your parents?

Do you take advantage of your parents' preference for you by asking for favors?

Do you say mean things to your parents about your sibling?

Do you participate or listen if your parents say unpleasant things about your sibling?

Have you acknowledged to your sibling that you are the favored one?

Are you ready to listen and understand your sibling's feelings about having to grow up seeing you as the favored one?

Do you expect favored treatment in love and work?

Do you find it difficult to give to others without expecting something back?

If you were not a favored child:

Do you feel anger and resentment toward your favored sibling?

Do you feel competitive with your sibling?

Are you still hoping you can win your parents' love?

Do you think you have done something wrong, or that your sibling is deserving of his or her favored status?

Do you blame your sibling for being favored?

Do you get involved in love or work relationships that repeat your relationship with your sibling?

The following anecdotes will illustrate some of the ways in which favoritism undermines the sibling relationship.

"They Like Him Better, There Must Be Something Wrong with Me": When Siblings Blame Themselves

If your parents favored your sibling over you, chances are you assumed that something was wrong with you instead of with your parents. I've never met a person who understood as a child that favoritism reflected a parental problem. In fact, I consider it a victory when a disfavored child realizes and accepts this in adulthood.

Some siblings try to justify their parents' feelings by agreeing that their sibling is indeed better than they are and deserves favored status. This is what happened to Kim, who entered therapy suffering from recurring bouts of depression. "Sometimes I stay in bed for days," she said at our first session. "I'm so unhappy and I can't see that it's ever going to change. I don't want to continue my life." When she wasn't depressed she would get involved with men who didn't value her. When each relationship ended, she would be thrown into another deep depression, thus continuing her cycle. She came to me as a last-ditch effort.

Within a few sessions I had learned a lot about Kim's family. Her brother, Neal, was three years older and her parents' favorite. Both Kim's parents had come from families that were partial to boys, and they carried that prejudice through to their own family. Kim's mother, in fact, still worshipped her older brother and held him up as a shining example for her son. Neal had been shuttled to and from Boy Scout meetings, football games, tennis practice, and track meets; his activities took so much time that there was none left over to take Kim to Brownies. Neal's mother often brought home clothes for Neal that she "just happened to see," while Kim got new clothes only in the fall and at Christmas. Whenever the two siblings fought, it was always Kim's fault. "You're just jealous of your brother," Kim's mother would claim. That was true, Kim said to me, she did feel jealous and that was wrong.

"Well, of course you felt jealous," I replied. "Your parents' favoritism made you feel inadequate around your brother."

"Oh, no," she said, "they didn't make me *feel* inadequate. Compared to my brother, I *am* inadequate." She went on to explain that Neal was handsome and brilliant and "destined for great things," as her father always said.

At this point I told Kim emphatically that her parents' favoritism toward her brother was the basis for her troubles in the present—her depression, her lack of self-esteem and self-confidence. All of her life, Kim had looked into the mirror and seen her parents' reflection of her; she never once saw her true self.

One session I asked her to bring in some pictures of Neal. I was not surprised to see that he was a regular-looking guy. Ironically, Kim herself was a black-haired, blue-eyed beauty whose drab clothes and sad eyes couldn't hide her attractiveness.

While we looked at the photos together, I asked Kim to describe Neal to me. She said he was tall, gorgeous, athletic, and had a winning smile. I pointed out that in fact he was of average height and moderately attractive. He did, I agreed, have a charming smile.

I also asked Kim to bring in a few photos of herself. The Kim she described was nothing like the beauty I saw in the pictures. Just as I had disputed her perception of Neal, I disputed her perception of herself; I told her how beautiful she appeared in the photographs and in person.

As Kim's relationship to herself improved, her relationship with Neal shifted. Whereas before she never talked about herself, she did now, and she quickly saw that he was disinterested. "I always thought it was because I had nothing to say, but even when I do, he doesn't listen," she said. She also became more assertive at work. Then, as was her pattern, she fell for a guy who didn't appreciate her.

In one session she recounted to me a painful episode with her boyfriend, where he had made fun of her in front of a bunch of his friends. "Maybe if you talk to Neal about your feelings, you won't have to act them out with other men," I suggested.

Scared by the prospect of sinking into her old depression, she decided to call her brother and ask him to come in for a therapy session. Neal was impatient with her, but agreed.

When Neal showed up, Kim said she wanted to talk about the favoritism in the family. He seemed a bit taken aback but didn't resist, and soon he was talking about how his parents "always seemed to find it easier to be with me."

"Did you wonder how Kim felt about that?" I asked.

He looked at Kim, then back at me. "It never bothered her," he said.

I hear this response frequently from favored siblings, by the way. In order to justify their favored status, they must deny their sibling's feelings. If Neal started feeling sorry for Kim, he would have to confront the unfairness of his parents' treatment.

"It *did* bother me," Kim said. "It hurt my feelings, it made me feel inadequate. I never knew what I had done wrong."

Neal looked like he had just been ambushed. "But you never sought out their attention," he said. "You were always so quiet, you just kept to yourself."

"I think I learned to be that way, Neal, because there just wasn't any attention for me to seek out. They weren't interested."

"Well, Jeez," Neal said, angry. "What do you want from me? It's not my fault. Why don't you drag *them* in here?"

"I want you to acknowledge that it was unfair," Kim said quietly.

Kim had hit a nerve. Neal knew his favored position was unfair, yet to admit it might mean he would have to do something about it. I watched Neal's self-confidence drain away. He didn't say anything for a long time. Then he shook his head. "I feel like shit," he said, looking pale. "I don't like this at all."

Finally he said, "Sure it was unfair."

"I know it wasn't your fault," Kim responded.

"But I feel bad now," he said. "I guess this is what I've been trying to avoid."

In order for Neal and Kim to even begin having an honest relationship, they had to reach this point. After that conversation, they got together several times and talked, not just about their family's dynamics, but about their jobs, their interests, and their friends. Slowly each began to discover who the other was.

In the process Neal began to open up to Kim; he told her what enormous pressures he had grown up with, being the favored son. His parents expected him to do better than anyone else. In order to hold on to their good feelings about him, he felt he had to be the best. He told Kim he never really enjoyed learning or doing; the outcome was all he was focused on—the best grade, the promotion, the right girlfriend, the accolades that would follow.

"I'm driven to succeed, but it's all external," he said. "Nothing feels good inside, because I can never rest, I have to go on to the next thing and prove myself worthy all over again."

Neal's parents made it difficult for him to relinquish his favored status. They were always tempting him with money, attention, and compliments. But now that he was more aware of Kim's feelings, he was not comfortable with the way they left her out. And, once he had voiced his own anger at the favoritism, his resentment surfaced. He asked his parents to stop pressuring him so much. They responded by fussing over him even more.

As Kim continued to explore how her parents' favoritism had affected her, she went through several months of feeling the anger and hurt that she had repressed. Once those feelings emerged, her depression began to lift. As she began to trust her perceptions more, she began avoiding people who didn't appreciate her, including her parents. She and Neal continue to work on their relationship, although for a while Kim found it hard to acknowledge that Neal too had difficulties with the favoritism.

What You Can Do

Look at photos of yourself and your sibling. Show the photos to a friend, therapist, or lover. Describe what you see, and find out whether your partner sees the same thing. If you were not the favored sibling, your image of yourself is probably as distorted as your image of your sibling. Listen to what your friend or therapist tells you. Learn to take in the positive things people say about you. Practice comparing what you see with what your friends see. Believe your friends, until you can accurately see yourself.

If you were the favored one, you may be perceiving your sibling as less attractive or special than you. Although painful, this photo exercise may be an eye-opening experience for you, as well.

In order for you and your sibling to begin having a relationship, both of you have to acknowledge the favoritism. This is often a major stumbling block for siblings. If you are the disfavored one, it may be hard to approach your sibling. Since you've been in a one-down position with your sibling all your life, talking about the situation may seem like a continuation of that pattern. But this is not the case. Talking about your feelings is empowering and never a sign of weakness.

It will be hard to hear your favored sibling tell you how she has been wounded by being favored. From your point of view, she has probably had a cushier life than you. Give yourself time to feel empathy. You don't have to rush.

As a favored sibling, you can initiate this conversation, as well. If your favored status is blocking the way of developing a relationship with your sibling, you may now be willing to give up some goodies in return for achieving that relationship.

"Mother Always Liked Me Best": When Favored Siblings Use Their Special Status

Parents who have been abused, neglected, abandoned, or betrayed by *their* parents often find their own children threatening. They may be afraid, for instance, that their children will gang up on them, talk behind their backs, or perhaps see through them and recognize how weak the parents really are. Insecure parents want their children to love them unconditionally.

Frequently, the result is that one or both parents pulls a child out of the pack and treats him as special to secure his loyalty. The next step is to strip away the power of the other children by demeaning them directly or to the favored sibling. When parents, on top of favoring one child, also model negative, abusive, or devaluing behavior toward their other children, the favored sibling often mimics that behavior.

Favored children from these kinds of homes often grow up as selfish, mean people with an attitude. They can be completely insensitive to their siblings' (and later, to others') needs. They will flaunt their special status, saying things to their siblings such as "Mother likes me best," or "Dad says you're a jerk," or showing off the latest toy, piece of clothing, or cash their parent has bestowed on them.

If you come from a family such as this, chances are your sibling will not respond to the kind of challenge that Kim issued to her brother. Your sibling may revel in her favored status and may lack any sense of how you feel. In that case your goal should be to extricate yourself from the relationship if your sibling is still in a position to hurt you or use you. The story of my client George is a good illustration of this solution.

George was the youngest of three children. Joseph, the oldest, was their mother's favorite. She treated Joseph more like a partner than a child. Their parents divorced when George was very young and their mother had never remarried. Joseph supervised George and his sister, Letti, while they did their chores. He was given the power to discipline them.

Their mother had been ridiculed by her own mother as a child. Walking into a room, her mother would stare at her and then turn to a friend or other family member and say, "Look at her," as if the girl were an object. "Look at the messy hair, those terrible shoes." Their mother often spoke of how awful it felt to grow up with such a cruel parent. But she said the same kinds of things to Joseph about her other children. Joseph was her friend, she told him in front of her other children, the one who would never ridicule her or hurt her. A few times George protested, "*I* would never hurt you, Mommy," but his mother just shrugged or turned away.

Joseph had little to do with his siblings. Although there was only two years' difference among the children, he never played with them, watched TV with them, or even talked to them as equals. Instead, if George was watching TV, Joseph would come in and change the channel to what he wanted to watch. If George complained, Joseph told him to leave the room or pushed him violently off the couch.

As an adult, Joseph was demanding and self-centered. On the rare occasions when he did see George or Letti, he talked nonstop about himself and never asked them about their lives. He would announce matter-of-factly how special he was, declaring, for instance, that he was a brilliant lawyer, a superb skier, or an incredible lover.

George too was an attorney. If Joseph needed any legwork done, he had his secretary call George to do it. Although George had enough work in his practice to keep him busy, he would drop everything to do the menial tasks his brother requested, because he was still anxious for Joseph's approval.

George's goal, he told me, was to confront his brother and demand that Joseph respect him. Then, George figured, he and Joseph could be friends.

I asked George what was driving him to have a relationship with a brother who treated him so disdainfully.

"He just has to see that I'm a good attorney, that I'm a good person, respected by others," he replied.

George's self-value hinged on getting his brother's notice. Because his mother had treated Joseph more like a partner than a child, George had seen his brother as a father figure, even though there was little difference in their ages. George had the same reaction to Joseph as children do to a distant, disapproving, cruel, or sarcastic father.

To George's dismay, I told him I didn't have much hope for his working out his relationship with his brother. When a brother or sister is as overbearing and superior as Joseph was with George, there's not much chance to develop a healthy adult relationship. In order to achieve that healthy relationship, Joseph needed to change. I didn't believe that Joseph would or could change, because his mother's treatment of him had so skewed his vision of himself and his siblings.

I suggested that George not accept any more work from Joseph, but occasionally he did, and each time George's self-esteem was battered. As he came to recognize this pattern, George learned to withdraw from Joseph. In the beginning, George had the fantasy that Joseph would notice that he wasn't taking the jobs or calling as he did before, and would miss his brother, feel bad, and reach out to him. After several months had gone by, George saw the truth—Joseph really didn't care. George was then able to let go of the last of his hopes for a relationship. George still sees Joseph infrequently, at family holiday gatherings, but by not putting himself in a position to be judged, he is able to maintain a safe emotional distance.

Changing Your Relationship

Recognizing what you can and cannot change is as important in a sibling relationship as in any other. Sometimes you have to cut your losses and let go. If your sibling behaves in ways similar to Joseph, then the relationship you have borders on (or is) abuse. The healthiest response is to place yourself in a position where you cannot be abused, and usually this means withdrawing from contact. Confronting someone like Joseph rarely succeeds because his self-centeredness runs so deep that he cannot hear or understand you. However, as you feel stronger, you may want to tell your sibling your feelings about the way he has treated you. But be clear about your reasons for doing so. If you still harbor even a tiny glimmer of hope that your sibling will finally come to respect or love you, sharing those feelings is not a good idea.

Take a close look at your other relationships to see if you are repeating any of the abusive aspects of your sibling relationship. Taking control of your sibling relationship will heighten your self-esteem, and eventually these positive feelings will permeate your other relationships as well, allowing you to take a stand.

If you are the favored sibling and you realize, through therapy or from relationships with others, that you have been harmed by being the favored one, it's never too late to tell your sibling you're sorry. Give some thought to how much of your favored status you would be willing to give up to have a relationship with your sibling.

"I Hate Her, She Stole All Their Love": Blaming the Favored Sibling

Rather than blaming themselves, as Kim did, some siblings blame the favored sibling. This approach feels safer than blaming the parents. But in order to begin healing your sibling relationship, you must come to understand that it is your parents who hold the key to your feelings. They allowed their needs to come first, to the exclusion of yours or your sibling's. This is a frightening thought for many people, as it was for Nadine.

Nadine was furious with her sister, Karen, for "stealing" all their parents' love. "Ever since we were kids," Nadine said, "she's pushed me out of the way to get them to focus on her."

I asked for examples from the present. Nadine said, "Okay. I fly all the way to Boise to visit. Karen insists on picking me up at the airport. Then she won't even let me spend five minutes alone with them. She's always hanging around. She has all these in-jokes with my mother about the neighborhood, stuff I don't know anything about, so I just sit there like an idiot while they blab on and on. I just hate her. And then what happens at dinner? We go to Karen's house, where everybody raves about what a great casserole she cooked, like she's a genius or something. And here I am coming all the way from L.A. with a new promotion, and they can't even ask about it because Karen's constantly in front of my face, waving herself around."

Nadine had similar trouble with the women in her office. Sure that they were out to get her, she secretly plotted ways to cause them trouble and to "show them up for what they really are." When it came to men, she was always falling for a guy who wasn't quite finished with an old girlfriend—or wife. She would be outraged as she reported the latest other woman's "manipulation." It never occurred to Nadine that the man was in any way responsible, just as it never occurred to her that her parents were responsible for the way they treated her compared to her sister.

When I suggested this connection to Nadine, she became enraged. A week later when she again talked about her boyfriend as an innocent, I told her firmly that she wouldn't be able to work out her current relationship if she didn't get her sibling-parental relationship in perspective. "That's where it all started," I said. "We have to look at it."

To make it easier on her, I suggested that on her next visit to Idaho she watch her sister and parents interact as if she were watching television. This would give her the objectivity she needed to see what was going on, and it would also temporarily shield her from feeling all of the pain at once. "Pretend it's not *your* family," I said.

When Nadine arrived in Boise, she tried observing her family dispassionately. She saw immediately that Karen didn't have to do anything at all to get her parents' attention. It began to register for Nadine that her parents had always favored Karen. She also began to notice Karen's efforts to be nice to her, efforts that she hadn't allowed herself to see before. She came back to Los Angeles confused and angry.

From a distance, Nadine began responding a little to Karen's overtures, answering Karen's cards or phone messages, things she had never done before. Karen became even more friendly. After a while, Nadine wrote Karen a long letter telling her how she felt about the favoritism in the family; how she used to blame Karen, but now saw that it was their parents who were to blame.

Karen phoned immediately after receiving Nadine's letter and said how relieved she was that Nadine could finally see what had been going on. She told Nadine that she had always been uncomfortable with the favoritism. It was so blatant, she told Nadine, and most of the time she would have preferred that her parents didn't fawn over her so much.

"I felt so humiliated," Nadine told me the next day. "All these years Karen saw me wanting what she was getting from my parents. How pathetic!"

"Not pathetic," I said. "Sad and hurtful. And it sounds like Karen paid a price, too."

Nadine started to cry. "But they love her more," she said.

"That's right, they do," I answered, "and there's nothing you can do about that. You can't change their feelings. Eventually you're going to have to accept that for what it is. You got a bum deal, but not from your sister."

Nadine finally allowed that it was her parents and not Karen who were the problem. But she also felt some justified anger toward Karen for accepting the favoritism. Although it's pretty unreasonable to expect that a child will turn down extras, it's not unreasonable to expect the other kid to be angry about it.

Karen listened to Nadine without being defensive and worked hard to make their relationship stronger. "I always wanted a sister I could be close to," she said to Nadine. "Being favored is nice, I can't deny that. And you're right, I didn't refuse their love. But being favored has its downside, too. Often I didn't enjoy the attention. I felt guilty and didn't really feel I deserved it over you."

Karen went on to confront her parents and rejected every attempt they made to favor her. If they offered to help her with a house payment, she asked if they had offered the same to Nadine. When they bought her clothes, she asked if they had sent clothes to Nadine. If they said no, Karen would either refuse to accept the clothes or would send half of them to Nadine herself. Her parents were at first confused, then they became angry. They thought Karen was being ungrateful for all the special attention they had given her. But Karen had made her choice. She chose her sister, now that her sister was open to her. It was up to their parents to adjust.

What You Can Do

If you, like Nadine, are having difficulty seeing what's really going on in your family, try observing them dispassionately as Nadine did. Pretend you're watching a television program, or are meeting them for the first time. This will allow you to see your family in a different light. How does your family interact? Where is the attention focused?

As the sibling of a favored child, you have undoubtedly felt unloved as you witnessed the attention your sibling received. Recognizing that this disparity is your parents' problem is hard. It is equally difficult to learn not to resent or to place anger on your sibling. Getting beyond all of these feelings is a big job.

Once you have sorted out the situation and accepted that your parents' problems are visited on you and your sibling, talk to your brother or sister about how you feel. It's natural to feel resentment or anger at your sibling for allowing herself to be favored. If you and your sibling are going to forge a relationship, you need to talk about your feelings about the favoritism.

If you are the favored sibling, you have not been taught to be sensitive to your sibling's feelings. But it's never too late to learn. Invite your sibling to talk about the situation you both grew up with. Ask about her feelings, and listen. Share your feelings too, and tell her what you are willing to do to make your sibling relationship work.

You will have to discuss how you will handle your parents' favoritism in the future. Karen confronted her parents and stopped accepting special favors from them. Many favored siblings are not willing to go this extra mile. You and your sibling will decide what's comfortable for both of you. Separating your relationship with your sibling from your relationship with your parents is essential. You and your sibling will have to discuss how to maintain your relationship separate from your relationship with your parents.

"I'll Be Better Than Him, Then They'll Love Me More": Sibling Rivalry

The child who reacts to a favored sibling by competing with him is hoping to change the parents' feelings by being better than the favored sibling. This is sometimes a mixed blessing. If you reacted this way, the competition has probably made you strong. By wanting to best your sibling, you avoided the victim or blaming role that many disfavored siblings take on. On the other hand, you're probably still trying to topple the golden boy or girl at work, or in some way to defrock people who have any kind of following or feeling of superiority. You may constantly challenge people and have a strong need to prove you're right, better, or smarter. However, it's only after you let go of the desire to please your parents that you can realize how strong you have become.

This is what happened to David. He and his younger brother, Evan, were born only 11 months apart; David could not recall a time when Evan was not there. Their parents had divorced when the boys were young, and David's mother had remarried when David was five. Their father was around for a few years after the divorce, but when he remarried, he and his new family relocated. Their stepfather never made an effort to get involved with either Evan or Dave. He traveled a lot, and his absences upset their mother, who was jealous and accusatory toward her husband.

Instead of dealing constructively with their problems, David's mother withdrew from her husband when he was home and focused her attention on Evan, who happened to look a lot like his father. Evan was pampered and spoiled and ultimately made into a wimpy little prince by his mother. Anything Evan did delighted her. "Oh, look at that, isn't he marvelous," she would say. When David did the same thing, he would barely get acknowledgment from her. David's response was to try harder.

"No matter what Evan did, I was determined to do it better," David told me. "Evan went out for track, so I went out for track. Evan played chess, I played chess. My goals were riveted on trying to beat him in every sport, in every class. And I did."

None of these accomplishments made a dent on David's mother. She still thought Evan walked on water. Her response to David was, "Well, of course you beat him, you're older." Several times she accused David of cheating. After a while, she even refused to watch the two boys compete.

As adults, Evan and David barely spoke to each other. Evan, 30, lived at home and did word processing for a temp agency, while David lived 2,000 miles away and had become a successful businessman. Whenever David visited, he was desperate for his mother's attention, boasting to her of what a great job he was doing or how much money he was making. All he received in return were disapproving comments about being a showoff. But he couldn't stop, he told me. "I see that look on her face, I hear her negative response, but I can't stop trying."

David's problems surfaced in his work. He openly vied for the attention of his boss and bragged about his accomplishments to anyone who happened to be within listening distance.

One day a woman he worked with said, "David, it's painful to watch you. In one way or another, you're always shouting, 'Please love me,' but nobody is listening."

At our first session David recounted his co-worker's words. "She was right, nobody listens," David said. "Until Lisa made that comment to me, I believed that if I just tried harder, my mother would notice. She never does."

David's self-esteem, his very personality, had been determined by his mother's favoritism. His problem was exacerbated by the fact that he had had no male figure in his life who showed an interest in him. David had to find out who he was. It was a long, difficult therapy, but David slowly let himself emerge and learned to resist the frantic urge to suck out all the attention he could get from everyone. He became involved with a woman who saw the softer side of him, and he eventually was able to be vulnerable with her. During one session he said, with great relief, "With her, for the first time, I feel like I don't have to prove myself every minute."

One day we talked about Evan. "I have no idea who my brother is," David said. "He's a symbol to me, not a real person." David called Evan at a time when he knew their mother would be out of the house, and told his brother that he would like to talk openly about their mother's favoritism and how it had affected both of them.

Evan was furious. "What are you complaining about? If Mom liked me better, it's because you brought it on yourself. You were always trying to beat me at everything, you were so competitive."

"Wait a minute," David had said. "I didn't pop out that way. I thought if I could show Mom I was as good or better than you, that she would love me like she loved you."

Evan said, "I don't have to listen to these accusations," and hung up the phone.

Evan wasn't willing or able to try to change his behavior, and David eventually stopped competing with him. The more accepting he became, the less defensive Evan was. What changed was David's view of the favoritism. "I've spent years feeling sorry for myself and jealous of Evan, but I can see now that he ended up getting the short end of the stick. Mother's favoritism made me strong. Obnoxious, but strong. It made Evan dependent."

Changing Your Relationship

Being the unfavored sibling may be the better position, as you can see from the example of David and Evan. By favoring a child, a parent often creates a dependent or weak individual like Evan. It's hard to see this if you need that love from your parents, but if you can step back and really analyze your situation, you may discover that you have had a favor done for you in not being favored.

But eventually you will still have to let go of the need to please your parents. This means accepting that you aren't going to receive the amount of love you want from them. Although this will be the most painful part of your healing, it's necessary for you in order to move on and become more healthy in all of your relationships. Be careful not to replace your parents' role with co-workers or partners who withhold love or approval. Try to seek out more accepting people, and believe them when they tell you that you are worthwhile.

Accept that your sibling has chosen to maintain a relationship with your parent rather than to begin a relationship with you. As long as this is your sibling's choice, you can't forge a relationship separate from your parents.

"It's All His Fault": Blaming the Black Sheep

Instead of singling out a child to favor, parents sometimes single out one to bear the responsibility for the dysfunction in the family. Parents may abuse this child physically or emotionally. They may dislike the child for some reason—she resembles the hated ex-spouse, she is less pliant, she represents personality traits a parent dislikes in herself or her partner, or she was born at the wrong time. Sometimes the mistreatment of one child is accompanied by favoritism of another child, but as often as not, the black sheep stands alone.

Black sheep view their siblings with a mixture of envy, anger, hurt, and shame. The black sheep's feelings are often reactive; how he feels about his siblings usually depends on how his siblings treat him. As adults, black sheep tend to repeat their parental and sibling relationships, becoming involved with people who either abuse them or feel sorry for them. Later, they may take their anger out on their own children by disfavoring one.

When one child is mistreated or disliked, all siblings are affected, just as they are when one child is favored. Siblings of black sheep respond to these situations in different ways. Some try to ignore it; some feel lucky not to be victimized themselves; some feel guilty; and some try to take the blame in specific situations in order to shield the sibling from their parents' anger. A few join in their parents' mistreatment.

As adults, children from such families cannot be neutral to black sheep they encounter out in the world. Out of feelings of guilt, they may involve themselves with people who need help, or they may be angry and abusive with people who remind them of their black-sheep sibling.

Sometimes siblings of black sheep express resentment toward the disfavored child for "bringing all the trouble" into the house. This reaction is almost always a cover for feelings of helplessness, as was true for Marjorie.

Marjorie was in a rage at Bob, her younger brother, who had been incessantly picked on by their father ever since he was born. Marjorie's mother left the room at the first sign of trouble between her husband and son. "Bob was always causing trouble, cutting classes, talking back to my dad, drinking," Marjorie said. "Our house was always in turmoil because of him."

Marjorie had difficulty empathizing with people who reminded her of her brother. Anyone who seemed the slightest bit rebellious or victimized made her angry. Victims of child abuse, she told me, "probably deserved it," just as women who were beat up by their husbands were "asking for it" and "probably liked it."

"So, you think Bob deserved the treatment he got from your father, that it was his fault?" I asked.

"Absolutely," she said.

One day I asked Marjorie, "What would happen if you were to sympathize with some of these people who make you so angry?"

"Ha!" she replied. "That will be the day."

"Well, let's just pretend. You're watching Bob being beat up by your father, again. You feel bad and want to help."

To my surprise, Marjorie broke down. "Oh God," she said, "there's nothing I can do. Nothing. Dad's so angry." She cried for a long time, a frightened, hiccuping kind of sobbing. Finally, when she stopped crying, she said, "It was awful, he was always yelling at him, hitting him. My father used to throw him up against the wall. I was terrified and I couldn't do anything. My own mother left the room, what could I do? I wanted

Bob to do something, to fix it, to make him stop, but he couldn't. Dad just never liked him and that's the truth. I don't understand how my father could do something so horrible as not like his own kid, but he did."

Marjorie's feelings of helplessness had converted to anger at Bob, and eventually at everyone else who was being abused or victimized in some way. Her helplessness was too painful for her to bear. The only way she could endure what was occurring was to blame her brother.

When Marjorie understood her own feelings, she called Bob. They had not spoken for several years. Her brother listened to what she had to say. Then he told her he wasn't interested in "rehashing my shitty life, just to make you feel better," and hung up the phone.

She waited a week and called him again. This time he stayed on the phone, but wouldn't let her speak. Instead, he blasted her with his anger for not helping him when they were kids.

She made herself listen. When he was done, she said, "Don't hang up." She told him she was sorry and she understood how he could feel that way, because she had felt the same way about herself. "I wish I could have made it different," she said, "but I was just a kid, too."

He was quiet on the other end of the phone. Then, after a moment, he hung up.

She called him every week for a while, and they finally agreed to get together. Bob's life was very different from Marjorie's. He was involved with drug dealers and drug users and used drugs himself. Marjorie had never even tried drugs. Nevertheless, it was clear to her when she visited her brother that he was glad to see her and wanted to make her feel comfortable.

"We have a long way to go," Marjorie said to me later. "On the one hand, I know I'm not responsible for something I couldn't control. At the same time I have these feelings that I should be able to save him single-handedly. I have to accept him where he is now, just as he has to accept me. At least we're trying to get to know each other, and that feels good."

Marjorie's softness began to emerge as she slowly resolved her sibling issues. She got involved with a man and for the first time, she told me, "I can listen to someone else saying they have a problem without getting that familiar knot in my stomach."

What You Can Do

If you're covering up your feelings of helplessness about the black sheep in your family with anger, this anger is surely spilling out into all your relationships. Once you identify and release your feelings, you will be more open to other people and less afraid of their pain.

If you are the black sheep, you may want to confront your siblings about their mistreatment of you. I suggest that you talk to a therapist or a very good friend beforehand, because you will need a lot of emotional support during this time. No matter how right you are, your siblings have been in a position to hurt you most of your life, and they may still hold more power to hurt you than you realize.

You may choose to distance yourself from your family and begin again. If you are still trying to please any member of your family or are taking any responsibility for your mistreatment, let go. None of the abuse you have received was deserved.

Avoid people who are like your parents or siblings, and be on the alert for your tendency to get involved in relationships where you repeat old patterns.

Favoritism in a family distorts and poisons the sibling relationship. It also creates problems for children out in the world, both for the favored and unfavored alike. Bridging the distance between you and your sibling and situating the problem where it belongs—with your parents—is a wonderful, positive first step.

If separating from a sibling is also necessary, doing so may be painful but is ultimately the most healthy response. Loving and believing in yourself may require that you walk away from an unhealthy relationship with your sibling. But with that act of emotional bravery, you have the opportunity to form more healthy relationships in the future.

CHAPTER SIX

"I'll Never Be as Successful as My Brother"

Resolving Competitive Feelings

Biblical stories, novels, movies of the week, newspapers, and tabloids are filled with gruesome tales about the sometimes murderous outcomes of sibling rivalry. The message, it seems, is that it's unhealthy, and sometimes downright dangerous, to compete with a sibling. Yet, at the same time, siblings are constantly pressured to compete, both within and outside the home, in everything from sports and academics to work and love. "Let the best man win" is our cultural motto, and siblings are not exempt.

Not surprisingly, unresolved competitive feelings that siblings harbor are among the most enduring obstacles in the way of resolving an adult sibling relationship. If you competed with a sibling as a child, you're probably still competing with your brother or sister today, as well as with other people in your life. Now, however, instead of competing for who has the better toys or more A's in school, you focus on who has the smarter kids, more money, prettier wife, better body, or better retirement fund.

Depending on the strength of your sibling relationship at home, you may have reacted to the competitive bait with indifference, or it may have made you crazy with jealousy or hurt. If you and your sibling had a close, connected relationship, you may have taken easy pride in her achievements, especially if you felt secure in your own. But if you and your sibling competed at home for your mother's or father's attention, then any attention she received in the outside world, good or bad, strained your relationship and fanned the competitive flames.

If you and your sibling managed not to get waylaid by societal or parental pressures, you may still have competed with each other for your own purposes. As we've seen, siblings constantly compare themselves to one another, figuring out their own identities by watching their siblings. Such comparisons often lead to competition and the attendant feelings of jealousy, anger, defeat, and resentment.

Hidden Competition, Open Competition

Depending on how you were raised, your competitive feelings are either overt or hidden. If you were raised to be the best, but your parents never said this to you directly, you and your siblings probably competed but were sneaky or slightly embarrassed about doing so. This covertness led to denial of competition. The denial, in turn, led you to act in ways that were (and probably still are) confusing to your sibling and to others. For instance, when Melissa and her sister go out to a bar and a man pays attention to Melissa, she demurs, but inwardly, she beams. If a man pays more attention to her sister, Melissa subtly criticizes him. Melissa can't admit to herself or her sister that she's competing; instead, she becomes critical. Her attitude creates distance and mistrust between the sisters.

In other families, siblings are encouraged to compete openly, and winning is the only important outcome. If your best wasn't good enough, then you learned that competition meant winning at any cost and that losing was a humiliation to be avoided. When Danny realized his brother Mel was going to pass him at a track meet, Danny tripped him. Mel tore a hamstring, Danny won, and his parents praised him. When Mel complained that Danny had tripped him, his father derided him for being a poor loser. Now Mel, too, plays to win; if someone is better, he plays dirty pool if that's what it takes to win. Verna, on the other hand, grew up in a similar family and feels so beaten by her older brother's achievements and personal success that she now avoids him altogether and shuns competition of any kind.

What all of these people have in common is that they don't know how to lose, or win, gracefully. They are outer-directed, paying more attention to what others have, worrying that someone else has it better, winning for the sake of winning, and valuing others' judgments of them rather than their own evaluations of themselves. Their self-value comes from beating their siblings and others; doing their best is not a motivating force.

Learning to be inner-directed—simply doing one's best and feeling good about it—is very difficult for people who are accustomed to unhealthy competition. If you have never used your own achievements as your gauge of success, but always looked outward to others, becoming inner-directed will be hard work.

Here are some questions you can ask yourself to determine if competition is still a major factor in your relationships.

Are you still competing for mom or dad's love, attention, and approval?

Do you still gauge your own achievements on the achievements of your sibling?

Do you want to show your sibling up?

Have you given up certain activities because your sibling was better at them?

Is your relationship with your brother or sister still based on trying to best each other?

Is what happens to your sibling sometimes more important than what happens to you?

Do you avoid competition?

Do you feel jealous or angry at your sibling because he has done well in something that was difficult for you?

Do you avoid people who perform better than you at certain tasks?

Are many of your relationships competitive?

As you read this chapter, you will see how others with similar problems have learned to face disappointment, set their sights on something realistic, and have come to know and understand their own limits and potential. I hope their stories will be helpful to you.

When Parents Generate Competition Between Siblings

Many parents, raised to compete with their own siblings and others, continue that competition through their children. Their own egos and their own self-worth become invested in their offspring. Not only do the parents have to win to look good, but their children must win too, since they are a reflection on their parents. Because they don't make a healthy separation between themselves and their kids, these parents experience their children's imperfect achievements as humiliating, and they take ownership of their children's positive achievements. For example, a friend of mine is a successful writer, but her mother rarely compliments her. Rather, her mother comments on how she instilled the desire to write in her daughter. When she talks to people about her daughter's achievements, she is really bragging about herself.

Parents who are quick to take ownership of their child's achievements are also quick to disown their failures. The child who succeeds is a "chip off the old block," but the child who fails is "lazy," "stupid," or "didn't take after either of us." Sometimes parents are so emotionally damaged that they feel rage and hate toward a child who doesn't function at the level at which they need him to function. These parents may cruelly withhold their love, or even physically harm their child for failing to perform to their satisfaction. If you were raised by such parents, you and your sibling may suffer from chronic anxiety and rage. You have, by necessity, become people pleasers, underachievers, or fierce competitors. Underneath all of these reactions lurks the horrible feeling that no matter how good you may be, you can be toppled or rejected at any moment.

When parents suffer from deep-rooted insecurities, they may encourage their children to fight for their attention because that is the only thing that makes the parents feel loved, needed, and important. If you were encouraged to fight for love and approval at home, then you undoubtedly took that style of being out into the world, and you now compete with friends, spouses, and co-workers. Since you have been trained to be outer-directed, winning is the only way you know to get attention, and approval and to feel good about yourself.

For instance, my client Joy's father encouraged her and her sister, Ann, to flirt with him, because their attention made him feel powerful and attractive. The daughter who was the most seductive with him received the most attention. This competitive tension followed Joy and her sister into their relationships with other women in adulthood. These sisters complained that women were threatened by them and were too competitive; both preferred the company of men. Each also repeatedly initiated affairs with married men. Although their primary relationships were with the men (who inevitably resembled their father), they were also in competition with these men's wives. In this way the sisters, as adults, continued to act out their early competitive feelings with each other. Only if a married man paid more attention to Joy or Ann than to his wife did the two sisters "win."

Raised to stroke their father's ego, Joy and Ann were deprived of the opportunity to be friends with each other or with any other women. They also viewed men as prizes to be won but never trusted.

"Daddy Loves a Winner": When Siblings Compete for Parental Love and Approval

When siblings take on fiercely competitive roles with each other, these damaging roles are usually resistant to change. Siblings raised to be brutally competitive have no trust to invest in each other, because showing a weak side is an unthinkable risk. Pleasing or getting the attention of a parent depends on beating the sibling; hence, your sibling is the enemy. My client Agnes and her sister, Mimi, were caught in such a trap with their father.

When I met her, Agnes had been trying for three years to have a child, but so far she and her husband had been unable to conceive. Their grief over their infertility was what brought them to couples counseling. Agnes's desperation was worsened by her sister Mimi's fecundity; Mimi had just announced that she was expecting her third child. Agnes was not shy about telling me how murderously angry and jealous she felt about her sister. She hated Mimi and wished bad things would happen to Mimi's kids.

When I asked whether Mimi had any idea Agnes was trying to have a child, she responded, "Are you kidding? Nobody in my family knows. Mimi would be disgustingly happy to find out that I wanted something she already has. She would torment me with my own pain."

Of all the events in Agnes's life, the ones that made her the most distraught, that made her doubt herself the most and feel the most self-hatred, were the events that happened to her sister, not to her. Her husband was focused on his own sadness and frustration about infertility.

110

But Agnes was almost exclusively focused on her rage at her sister for having something—babies—that she couldn't have.

Their father was an angry, perfectionistic dictator, while their mother was an ineffectual and fearful mouse. Their father's favorite motto was "Daddy loves a winner," the same thing his own father had said to him and his brother when they were growing up. He and his brother were bitter enemies, but he had never realized that they were enemies because their father had raised them to be.

Agnes's father demanded that his girls compete at every level: school, sports, popularity, looks. He praised the winner of each competition and taunted the loser unmercifully. Since he was still competing with his brother, if his brother's children did better than his daughters in anything, he went into a rage at Agnes and Mimi about how they were letting him down. To gain his attention and love, they had to win. When they looked at each other, they looked into the eyes of the enemy. They wanted to know the fears, insecurities, or worries of the other for one reason only: to exploit them.

These women were trained to compete not just with each other, but with the world. Constantly on guard, Agnes trusted no one. She made enemies at work and trampled on whomever she needed to "get the job done." Agnes suffered from ulcers and insomnia. The only time she could relax was with her husband, a man who felt no need to compete and who loved her unconditionally. Her husband's love allowed the softer, childlike side of Agnes to emerge.

When Agnes finally got pregnant, she realized that if her competitive feelings with her sister were not resolved, she and Mimi would carry on their competition through their children, just as her father and uncle had done. It was the love she felt for her unborn child, and her understanding of what had happened in her family, that made her want to break free from the death-grip her father had on both her and Mimi.

The first step she needed to take was to remove herself from the triangle that consisted of her, Mimi, and her father. One day Agnes said to me, "Okay, I'm ready. I concede my father's love to Mimi." Then she cried for a long time. This was difficult and painful, but it was the only way for Agnes to stop competing with Mimi for her father's attention and approval. She took herself out of the competition.

Initially she felt a "tremendous emptiness," as she put it. But as time went on she learned to fill that space by becoming inner-directed, paying attention to her own successes, not her sister's or someone else's. This step is an enormous one for any person who has spent a lifetime vying for the attention and love of a parent.

Next, Agnes wrote a letter to Mimi telling her what she had discovered about the nature of their competition with each other. Agnes wrote that she hoped that someday they could stop the destructive part of their relationship. Although she tried not to be competitive, the letter seemed to say that she'd seen the light before Mimi. Still, it was a beginning, because she had never told Mimi anything she was feeling before.

Mimi sent the letter back with the one lone typo circled in red and the words "Get real" written at the bottom. She then filled the back page with her latest "good news."

Agnes and I discussed how important it was for her to act on her new feelings, because Mimi was determined to maintain the relationship as it was. The first thing Agnes had to learn was not to jump to the bait. When Mimi bragged about her husband, house, or kids, Agnes needed to stop herself from responding with something bigger and better. The first time Agnes actually said "That's nice"—even though she didn't quite mean it yet—instead of instantly discounting what Mimi said, she knew she had come a long way. As part of her decision to distance herself from the competitive family triangle, Agnes also stopped flying to her parents' home in Denver for visits and holidays. Instead, she invited her parents and Mimi to visit her separately in Los Angeles.

For a while Mimi intensified her efforts to reengage Agnes in their competitive dance. It was clear that Agnes's new way of being was anxiety-provoking for Mimi. But Agnes got very good at responding positively and avoiding competitive conversations.

Now that her son has been born, Agnes has grown much happier, and is still determined to raise her little boy differently than she was raised. Mimi still calls and tries to pull her into the old game by bragging about her own kids, but less often than before. "I still cringe," Agnes said to me, "and I frantically run through what my kid has done lately, but Mimi doesn't know that I'm still doing that. And I see how destructive it is."

Mimi has been unwilling to let go of her competition with Agnes. Until she does, Agnes knows she must keep her distance from Mimi. Getting their father out of the picture was the essential key for Agnes, and she remains open to beginning a new relationship with her sister. But, as Agnes says, "There is probably just too much water under the bridge. We've spent our whole lives despising each other. That might not be possible to reverse."

Changing Your Relationship

If your sibling relationship is similar to Agnes and Mimi's and you want it to be different, pulling out of the competition is probably your healthiest, albeit frightening, alternative. Attempting to talk with your sibling, trying to elicit support, or instigating a truce is likely to cause only suspicion. After all, you and your sibling have no basis from which to trust each other yet, so it's going to be important for you to follow through with actions, like Agnes did.

Don't respond to your sibling's jabs or attempts to hook you into competing; resist the urge to throw a recent promotion or your kid's tennis trophy in your sibling's face. Your sibling will eventually notice your behavior has changed. It takes two to carry on the kind of competitive derby you and your sibling have had up until now. When you disengage, the old maneuvers your sibling attempts will seem distant, even slightly sad.

Only after your sibling sees that she cannot engage you in a competitive dialogue, and only after you have stopped fighting over your parents' attentions, will your sibling begin to trust that you are sincere. These changes, even if they are slow to modify your sibling relationship, are guaranteed to make your future relationships closer and less provocative, and to allow you to begin to know others as friends rather than rivals.

Your sibling may intensify her efforts to pull you in, and may become more aggressively combative or hostile. If, after some time, your sibling doesn't come around and continues to be abusive, the healthiest alternative may be to avoid contact with her. Tell her, in a letter or in person, why you are withdrawing from the relationship. If you see her at family functions, don't engage in old behaviors with her. This will be difficult, because she will try any tactic she can think of to pull you back in, but hold your ground. The competitive, hateful urges she elicits from you will fade once you leave, and you will feel stronger each time you resist.

"We Were Competitors for a Scarce Commodity": When There's Not Enough Love to Go Around

If parents spend little time with their children, or pay them little attention, the children often end up in competition for the scarce commodity of parental love. Even if the parents don't encourage competition, the children often blame one another for the dearth of affection they feel, rather than understanding that there just wasn't enough love in the home to begin with. As adults, these siblings are quick to blame others for their problems. They can be brutal or manipulative when it comes to getting whatever attention is available from the world at large or within adult relationships. This is what happened between my client Anthony and his younger brother, Thomas.

Anthony sought therapy to work on his temper. He threw tantrums on the squash court when he was losing, screamed obscenities at his opponent, sulked and banged balls off the wall, sometimes barely missing his opponent. When he won, he was equally abusive in his boasting and bragging. He had no male friends, and his relationships with women were punctuated by demands for attention and outbursts of jealous rage.

As we talked about his family history, a clear picture of parental neglect emerged. Anthony's parents paid little attention to him or Thomas throughout their childhood. Most of the time the two children were cared for by nannies and housekeepers. When their father or mother would "stop in" to visit, both boys grabbed things to show them, shouting at each other to shut up and pushing each other out of the way. Within minutes of the parents' arrival, the two boys were screaming at each other, trying desperately to get the attention of their by now annoyed parent, who invariably walked out within another minute or so. The two boys would then fall into angry accusations about who had made their mother or father go away.

As adults, both men were needy and constantly fought for the attention of others. For Anthony, there was never enough love; he never enjoyed what he had, because he was always fearful that it would vanish. His wife threatened divorce because she said he either frightened her with his jealous, possessive rages or pushed her away with his derogatory comments about her looks or intelligence.

During the next several months while Anthony was in therapy, he had the opportunity to visit his parents and Thomas twice. During these visits, Anthony finally realized how unavailable and disinterested his parents were toward both of their sons. It pained him to recognize how he and Thomas continued desperately to seek their approval, to no avail. Anthony changed dramatically when he returned from the second visit.

"That situation," he said to me, "is very clear-cut. It's like a curtain has parted. I see it all differently now. I see my parents for who they really are, and it hurts a lot."

Although Anthony now clearly understood why he and Thomas had acted as they did toward each other, he still held on to his dislike and his angry feelings. "Seeing Thomas now is like looking into a mirror," he said. "I see the part of me that I don't like: the neediness, the anger."

Anthony focused on trying to make changes in his current personal life, but it wasn't easy for him to change his whole mode of being overnight. While struggling to get close to others, he constantly caught himself one-upping another person or blaming others for his difficulties. He had to struggle to keep from exploding when he watched his wife simply talking to another man, and he had to fight his urge to push her away when she returned to him. His wife was patient; as long as he was trying to change, she was willing to stay with him.

What You Can Do

If you are accustomed to pushing others out of the way, or do not trust the constancy of love, you too will have difficulty as you try to change your behavior. One of the techniques you can use is to stop yourself before an angry or jealous outburst. Ask yourself what you are really feeling. Chances are you are probably feeling frightened and needy. You are probably terrified that your loved one will find someone better and leave you. Try to express these fears directly to your spouse or friend. Because of your hostile relationship with your sibling, you probably won't feel comfortable expressing these feelings to him for some time. Focus, for the time being, on your more current relationships.

Your next, most difficult step will be learning to comfort yourself when you feel angry, jealous, or insecure. For now, work on letting others come close to you, without clinging to them or pushing them away. For instance, Anthony learned not to make sarcastic remarks when his wife said something nice to him, and this change allowed her to grow closer to him, bit by bit. With practice, he too felt closer to her.

When you're ready to work on changing your relationship with your sibling, focus on the previous example of Agnes and Mimi and try some of the approaches Agnes took. For instance, write or talk to your sibling about your relationship, disengage from competing for your parents' attentions, and learn to respond positively to good news from your sibling.

When Siblings Generate Their Own Competition

If you and your sibling both liked the same sport, class, or friend or had the same ambition, you probably ran into head-on competition and knotty interpersonal problems. If each of you was lucky enough to have a separate interest, some activity in which you excelled, your competitive feelings may have been mitigated. If your sibling had all the luck—

good grades, looks, friends—you probably either felt defeated, angry, and resentful, or you worshipped your sibling like a god and avoided competitive situations altogether.

Competition with a sibling is often painful. If your brother was a sports hero in school and you were not, you had to face your own limitations as well as the achievements of your sibling. Discovering your own limitations is a necessary part of growing up, and the way these delicate, hurtful matters are handled in childhood determines how you handle defeat or success in adult life. As a kid, you either supported your brother or despised or competed with him. As an adult, these responses and feelings have followed you into your other relationships. You may, for instance, be adept at avoiding people who are superior to you in some task. You may have a chip on your shoulder about superachievers, or you may despise competitive people. If you couldn't find an area in which you could successfully compete with your sibling, you may feel generally defeated. As you'll see in the next anecdote, defeated siblings often become underachievers and carry the burden of resentment, jealousy, and low self-esteem with them into the world.

"I'll Never Be as Successful as My Brother": The Defeated Sibling

Lee was a solid B student, and his younger brother, Richie, always got A's. It didn't matter to Lee that his parents praised him for his grades and never compared him to Richie; he still felt the sting of his brother's better grades.

As youngsters, Richie and Lee had fun together and cooperated on projects, but once Richie started school and clearly excelled, Lee pulled away. He distanced himself from Richie by maintaining a sarcastic older brother stance. For a few years Richie tried to get Lee to like him again and to pay attention to him, but he gave up by the time he got to high school.

In college, Lee put out the best effort he could and ended up with a B+ average, the best he had ever done. When Richie took the same business courses three years later and aced every one of them, Lee's competitive feelings turned to defeat, rage, and jealousy. He became even more sarcastic toward Richie and began to talk openly about what a stupid person his brother was and how much he disliked him and his "earnestness."

It had been assumed that both sons would enter their father's business after college, but Lee surprised everyone by moving to Southern California the day after he graduated. He rented an apartment near the beach and took up surfing. He spoke contemptuously about people who "did the corporate thing." Because Lee was unable to resolve his competitive feelings and felt defeated, he rejected the whole package—not just his brother, but also the business world his brother would soon inhabit.

When I first saw Lee in therapy, he came across as bitter and resentful. He had run into trouble with cocaine and alcohol, and his girlfriend had convinced him to get some therapy. He hid behind a fatalistic view of life. He would say things like, "Why should anybody try, when the world might blow up tomorrow?" By this time, he had kicked around Southern California for three years doing odd jobs and spending most of his days surfing. He mythologized about "living life on the edge," but he was lost, drifting with no purpose. At his girlfriend's and my urging, he began going to A.A. meetings as well as coming to therapy sessions.

When I asked about his relationship with his brother, it was as if I had touched an exposed nerve. His pain was clear. The life he had been living was a thin cover for his feelings of defeat and humiliation.

Although his family had been supportive of Lee, they had not been prepared to handle the unforeseen circumstance of the younger brother eclipsing the older. Lee's parents could see his pain but had no idea how to help.

Lee foresaw nothing but problems if he joined his father's business. He couldn't stand the thought of a constant competition that he would always lose. "What was going to happen when Richie and I took over the business?" Lee asked me. "Would my brother be president because he got A's in accounting? And why should they make me president just because I was older?"

Since no one had ever discussed how the future was going to be, Lee had made his own decision to bail out and became a surf bum.

Lee, however, discovered that he liked the business world. After he conquered his alcohol and drug problem, he applied to an MBA program and got a job with a small but expanding film distribution company.

His parents were delighted that he was getting his life together, but his father remained hurt that Lee had rejected the family business. Lee explained to his parents why he had not joined the family business and why he had been sidetracked for those few years.

"They really had nothing to say," he told me. "I can see now how uncomfortable they are with feelings, theirs and mine."

The hardest part of Lee's healing was talking to Richie, because he felt like he was already at a disadvantage. Lee received a lot of support from his girlfriend, his sponsor at A.A., and me. He was strong enough, he realized, to admit his feelings of inadequacy.

Richie was shocked at what Lee had to say. He had looked up to his older brother and believed Lee's rebel stance. He had no idea that he had had an influence upon Lee's choices. Richie didn't feel he had eclipsed his brother at all. He just figured his brother was ultra-cool and was doing something Richie would never have the nerve to do: chucking everything to go surfing every day. Richie also said that he had always assumed his brother could do anything, including getting A's if he wanted to.

Although Richie was surprised, he never denied Lee's feelings. Intuitively Richie did the right thing by accepting them. When Richie was made president of their father's company, Lee had to accept that reality. Until Lee could feel that he was successful in his own right, however, he could not fully accept his brother's success. Fortunately, as Lee developed his own standards for success and became more inner-directed, he began to feel good about his accomplishments. He learned to focus more on what *he* was doing rather than on what his brother or anyone else was doing. When he received his grades or a promotion at his job, he would first ask himself if he had tried his best. If the answer was yes, he forced himself to feel good about the result, whether it was an A or a C. Eventually he did not have to force these feelings.

Changing Your Relationship

The more you can focus on your own life, the less hurt you will be by what you perceive as your sibling's greater success. Like Lee, developing your own standards of success is imperative, not just for a more healthy sibling relationship, but for a more balanced, healthy relationship with yourself and everyone else in your life.

If your sibling tells you that he has had competitive feelings toward you, listen to him with respect. Don't make jokes or try to tell him he doesn't feel as he does. Your sibling is revealing his sense of inadequacy to you, an admission that takes courage and deserves respect from the listener.

Your relationship may be complicated by the power of the older/younger sibling roles, a common occurrence. Younger siblings often don't think their older siblings could possibly be threatened by them. If you are a younger sibling, be alert to this possibility and ready to listen to your older sibling. By acknowledging this part of your relationship, you can equalize your sibling relationship into one of two adults, rather than the old roles of older/younger siblings and all the attendant expectations.

"He Doesn't Know I'm Competing with Him": When Competition Is Underground

Often siblings have ambivalent, confusing feelings about their competition with a brother or sister. For instance, when older siblings are helpful and pleasant to a younger sibling, the younger sibling may feel guilty for and afraid of his or her competitive feelings. Sometimes girls are told it's not ladylike to compete with their brothers, or are urged to compete in areas that do not overlap their brothers' activities.

By exhibiting competitive feelings, siblings fear they might lose the friendship of their older sibling—or, worse, that their sibling might laugh at or dismiss them. Many siblings bury their competitive feelings and never let them surface. This is what happened with Joan and her older brother, Freddie.

When they lived at home, Freddie, older by three years, was Joan's enthusiastic companion. He took her to the movies with his friends, affectionately teased her, and helped her with her homework. Freddie was smart, got A's in most subjects, went on to medical school, and became a teaching physician at Harvard. Joan struggled with her feelings, because she felt both a desire to beat Freddie and, at the same time, pride that he was doing so well. Joan never let on that she felt competitive with her brother, because she was afraid of losing his friendship. She also thought that admitting her competitive feelings would make her look foolish, because Freddie was such an achiever.

Internally, however, she measured her progress to his; everything she accomplished was filtered through her brother's accomplishments. She graduated in the top third of her class at UCLA law school, but Freddie had been in the top 10 percent of his graduating class, so in her own eyes she had failed. Although competitive feelings affected her interactions with everyone she knew, they were entirely underground. In fact, she often said that she was not a competitive person by nature, and nothing in her behavior would make anyone think otherwise.

When her brother or a colleague bought a new home, or a friend's child was accepted at a prestigious private school, she was sweet and congratulatory, but inside she felt the smile was frozen on her face. She would lie awake in bed that night with a sinking, sick feeling, wondering if she would ever catch up, if she would ever be good enough, trying to calm the fear that people were pulling ahead of her—that she was hopelessly behind.

When she heard bad things about her brother or anyone who ranked above her in any way, one of her first reactions was, "Ah, now I can pull ahead." She felt ashamed of these feelings, yet couldn't stop them. She couldn't share them with anyone until she came into therapy and they spilled out.

All of her relationships, she told me, were phony, because no one knew what she was really like. Underneath, she said, lived a horrible person who reveled in the failures of others and who wanted to win at all costs. She was so good at her deception, she told me, that she was usually the first person her brother called to tell his good or bad news, because he believed she was 100 percent behind him.

"And I *am* happy for him," Joan said. "It's just that I have these other, awful feelings too."

Joan's parents had made a big point of teaching their children that family was what counted. Friendships are great, they would say, but it's always your family that you can count on. She felt guilty for her competition with her brother. He had always been so nice to her, so much in tune with her parents' beliefs about supportive family relationships. In order to deal with her feelings, Joan had had to polarize herself; she felt her competitive feelings were all bad and so she pushed them underground. Her "good" self was never competitive. In fact, she denied having any competitive feelings.

With a lot of practice and prodding in therapy, Joan gradually discovered her own priorities. She discovered, for one thing, that teaching was more interesting than her private law practice. In fact, she hated practicing law and realized she did it only to make money, because her brother made a lot of money. Eventually she came up with new goals for herself and gradually phased out of her private practice to focus on her academic career.

Her husband gave her a hard time initially. A "dyed-in-the-wool Yuppie," as he described himself, he was frantic that without Joan's considerable income they would "lose their edge." Joan's husband was making her changes even more difficult by tweaking her insecurities about her "bad" competitive self. During this time, she realized that her husband, who craved success, had been her cover. On the surface, he was the one who pushed to get ahead while she pretended not to care, and if she talked about her success at all she said it was "important for Doug."

Joan was determined to overcome her past. As time went on, she felt better and stronger about her decisions. Then came the biggest surprise:

she had never wanted children, but now she changed her mind.

"There was something so horrible about those secret feelings I had that I was really afraid to pass them on to my children. I didn't want them to be as driven as I was," Joan said. "But now that's fading. I feel more confident now. I don't believe I'll pressure my children to succeed so that I look good. Now I trust that I can be a good parent."

In the spring, she and her husband visited Freddie in Boston. As Freddie gave them a tour of his new home, Joan suddenly said, "This is a great house. It's reactivating all my competitive feelings, Freddie."

Her brother just stared at her, then laughed and moved on down the hallway toward the next room. "Right, Joanie," he said.

"I'm serious," she said. "I've always felt competitive with you. I just never admitted it."

Her brother stopped and looked back at her. "You're kidding," he said quietly.

That night, she and Freddie stayed up till 3:00 talking. The following week, she told me how free she finally felt. "It was like a soul colonic," she said, laughing.

What You Can Do

For Joan, admitting her competitive feelings was a relief. Initially, you may feel too vulnerable to admit those feelings to your sibling. What made it possible for Joan to do so was her burgeoning sense of self-worth and self-confidence because of her acceptance of her competitive feelings.

If competition with your sibling has been what has spurred you on, your next step is accepting that *your* best is what's important, not your sibling's best. When you stop comparing yourself to your sibling and using him as your measuring stick, you will eventually feel proud of your own accomplishments. Try to be honest and accepting of your abilities and liabilities; we all have both. Set reasonable goals for yourself based on your experience.

Reward yourself for a job well done. Acknowledge your competitive feelings and express them; then try to let them go. Don't imagine yourself a bad person because you feel competitive with your sibling and others. Try to understand what it is about your family that helped to form the feelings you now have. When you're ready, you can tell your brother or sister how you feel and clear the air.

"We Were on Two Ends of the Same Canoe": When Survival Is More Important Than Competition

The only antidote I've noticed for unhealthy competition between siblings is a dysfunctional family: parental instability often creates intensely loyal sibling relationships. I'm not recommending this as a solution to sibling rivalry, because powerfully bonded relationships such as these come with a price tag. This antidote, while preventing unhealthy competition, also prohibits normal competitive reactions as well. An example from my family might help to explain what I mean.

I never felt competitive with either of my siblings. The age difference between Harry and me (I'm nine years older), as well as the difference in sex and our divergent interests, made competition less likely. My parents gave him more positive attention and more material things, but I felt parental toward Harry myself. I hoped that Harry would make my parents happy.

In contrast, my relationship with my sister, Joanne, was ripe for competition. We were close in age and the same sex. People were always comparing us, and Joanne had been proclaimed special by just about everyone. In another family setting I might have hated her, but I always felt close to her and she to me. Fortunately, I had a few achievements under my belt—like skipping second grade, being the favorite slave to the nuns at school, and being a super softball player—that might have made her feel competitive, too.

When I brought up the topic recently, Joanne said, "Oh no, we never competed, we always stuck together; we were on two ends of the same canoe." That was a good way of putting it, for if Joanne and I had competed, we would have run the risk of losing each other, or capsizing our boat, a prospect that terrified both of us. Ultimately, it didn't matter how other people labeled us, how they defined us, or who they favored; we were a team, and our relationship to each other was more important than anything else.

In our troubled family, the relationship between Joanne and me was the only stable force, the only relationship that could be trusted. If I competed with my sister, I might lose her as an ally. Unconsciously I must have reasoned that competition was dangerous and I was wise to avoid it. I never competed with other girls in high school for a boy's attention—or, when I got older, with other women for a man's attention. In school, I hid my intelligence because I didn't want anyone to "feel bad." I would sense the area in which a person was vulnerable—looks, personality, or intelligence—and go out of my way to offer a compliment. Whenever I felt anyone was competing on any level with me, I either withdrew or I let that person know I thought they were great—in other words, I let them win.

I also believed I must constantly reassure Joanne, compliment her, and shore up her confidence. In fact, this is what I found myself doing with everyone: I made sure they were okay so that I would be okay. Joanne and I were outer-directed, but with a different twist. We weren't judging our own success based on the failure of the other, or striving to do better than the other. We were watching to make sure the other was on her feet. The better my sister did, the safer I was, and vice versa. But we had to remember that we couldn't be too good, because then we might engender competition. Very tricky!

When I was in my early twenties, I realized that my inability to compete was getting in my way. I was an underachiever, afraid to explore my potential. By examining in therapy my family's dynamics and my own problems in living, I discovered why I reacted to others as I did. Seeing that the roots of my fear were based in my past gave me the courage to change my behavior in the present. Change was frightening in the beginning, because I felt so exposed, but eventually my fears subsided and I felt proud when I returned to school and excelled. I even won tennis matches without worrying about my opponent too much. Without the frantic need to shore each other up all the time, Joanne and I were finally able to talk about the real problems and worries in our lives. This frankness had been missing in our relationship because, as with many siblings in dysfunctional families, we counted heavily on each other and didn't want to upset or scare each other by sharing our vulnerabilities.

Also, and equally important, I didn't lose my sensitivity to others. I'm still complimentary, empathic, and supportive, because that's the kind of person I am. Those same qualities, however, are expressed in a pure way now, without my fears overlaying them.

What You Can Do

When siblings are dependent on each other for emotional or physical survival, then the confidence level of one's sibling becomes more important than one's own. My experience of relationships such as these is that the siblings' commitment to each other runs so deep that exploring the depths of the relationship will only expand and strengthen it. This may feel like a risk, but the strong sibling relationship will not be threatened by talking about things such as competition. The discussion may be uncomfortable at first, but I urge you to do it. You already have the beginnings of a powerful sibling relationship, but your childhood problems are still in the way of moving your relationship into the present.

Confront your own fear of competition and achievement. Keep telling yourself that any success you have will not harm anyone you love or who loves you. Force yourself to take pride in your achievements. Don't downplay your successes, don't make excuses for doing well, don't hide your abilities. Try poking your head up above the crowd. At first you will feel uncomfortably visible, but there's a lot of fresh air up there!

Encourage your siblings to do the best they can, for themselves. Discuss this with one another. Talk openly about your interdependence.

Compete with one another in small ways, for fun. For instance, play some games—checkers, tennis, footraces, jacks—and agree that who-ever wins will deliberately gloat and whoever loses will deliberately moan and whine. Lay it on thick and have fun. This exercise will help you and your siblings to playfully expose your fears and bring you even closer.

Breaking the bonds of destructive competitive relationships is not easy, but it can be done. Even in the worst cases, even if your sibling relation-ship has been poisoned beyond redemption, you still have the opportu-nity to change yourself and your future relationships.

Often, views about competition are generational. There's a good chance that what your grandparents believed about competition was passed on to your parents, and your parents passed these same, unexam-ined notions on to you. By coming to terms with your own problems and recognizing your parents' weaknesses in these areas, you will be on your way to fostering healthier attitudes about competition in your children.

CHAPTER SEVEN

The Parent-Sibling Vise

Stepping Out from Between Your Parents

The most stable families are those in which the boundaries between parents and children are clearly drawn. In these families the parents keep their spousal relationship separate from their relationship with their children, and they work out their differences together without involving their children. Too often these boundaries are blurred, however, especially when the relationship between the parents is shaky. Parents who are no more than children themselves; or parents with insecurities, fears, and unexpressed anger they haven't worked out yet; parents who don't know how to talk about their feelings in a healthy way; these parents rope their children in to their spousal conflicts. Then the parent-child roles become topsy-turvy, with children parenting their parents and becoming involved in the spousal relationship.

If your parents were not equipped to handle their conflicts or their emotions, chances are they recruited their children to resolve, mediate, or deflect their conflicts for them. In the process, you and your siblings stepped into certain roles. Perhaps you and your sister joined forces to mediate your parents' arguments or to side with one parent over the other. Your roles were compatible, and to this day you probably feel like a team, close and mutually dependent. On the other hand, perhaps you and your brother sided with opposite parents or fought with each other to deflect your parents' attentions from each other. Your roles were disruptive to your relationship, and as adults you and your brother are probably still contentious, angry, and distant with each other.

Whether the role you chose was compatible or disruptive, as an adult you may find it difficult to be genuine with your sibling or anyone else, because as a child you did not have the freedom to focus on your own needs. If you rescued your mother from your father's rage, you may now fall into the trap of rescuing others, including your siblings, and find it difficult to share your own feelings or problems. If you spilled your milk or banged your brother over the head with a toy every time your parents started to fight, you may still react anxiously to any hint of tension between other people. Those around you may mistake this reaction as selfishness or a desire for attention. If you mediated your parents' arguments, you may now find yourself putting aside your own needs, no matter how pressing, for the needs of others. These are just some of the ways in which children obliged to parent their parents carry their burdens into adulthood.

If your parents couldn't handle conflict without your help, they couldn't possibly have modeled for you how to resolve conflicts with your siblings or discuss angry feelings in a productive way. Now you may find it difficult to cooperate effectively with co-workers or to be close to those you love.

Following are some questions to help you discover if you are still tuned in to your parents' or others' conflicts.

Do you and your sibling spend most of your time talking about your parents or another sibling?

Do you feel compelled to fix your parents' relationship?

Do you worry that your sibling is causing problems for your parents?

Do you wish your sibling were more sensitive to your parents' needs?

Are your siblings putting pressure on you to behave in a certain way?

Are you in a relationship now that mimics your role at home?

Do you focus your attention on the needs of others?

Do you feel anxious or frightened when your parents argue?

Do you take sides when your parents have an argument?

As the examples in this chapter illustrate, it's well worth your while to learn for yourself what your parents failed to teach you while you were growing up. Only by understanding how you and your sibling fit into the parental vise will you be able to disengage from it and have a healthier, fuller relationship with your sibling and others.

Compatible Roles

When siblings adopt compatible roles to cope with parental conflict, they often describe their relationship as close, loving, and loyal. Because they are joined in a single goal—to keep their parents together—they depend upon each other. Most siblings in this situation believe they have a great relationship, but in fact they barely know each other.

What they do know is the intimate details of their parents' relationship, all the subtleties of gesture, the asides, the words that say one thing but mean another. This shared knowledge forms the basis for their relationship. When it comes to sharing details of their own lives and expressing their own feelings, siblings are at a loss.

If you recognize yourself and your sibling in this description, you probably have a "very nice relationship." Chances are you don't express anger, frustration, or hurt about your own life or your relationship with your brother or sister—at least not directly. The relationship between my client Miriam and her sister, Helen, is a good example of how these limits are set in place.

"Without Us Around, They Would Probably Kill Each Other": When Siblings Take On the Burden of Their Parents' Conflicts

Miriam, in her mid-thirties, came into therapy because she was afraid she was "going crazy." "All these angry thoughts keep popping into my head," she said at our first meeting. "Sometimes I want to throw things or scream, and I don't understand why, because everything is fine. I worry about my parents because they fight so much, but that's all."

Miriam, like many children who are caught in their parents' drama, had buried her own anger and her own needs in order to function as a mediator for her parents. But the anger she felt at being caught in this sticky web was beginning to surface, and Miriam didn't have a clue as to the origin of her anger.

Miriam and Helen's parents had picked at each other constantly when the two girls were growing up, and their fights escalated on occasion into physical abuse. Afraid of intimacy, Miriam's parents didn't know how to be close, and their anger functioned to keep them at a safe distance from each other. Since they had never learned how to resolve angry feelings, they involved their girls in their conflicts, and the two sisters did their best to help their parents bridge their angry feelings.

As children, the two sisters had hovered over their parents waiting for signs of distress. When an argument started they would try to change the topic or plead with their parents to calm down. But their mother and father kept fighting, until finally their father would storm out of the house. Miriam would jump up and follow him out, trying to talk him into returning home, while Helen would stay at their mother's side to talk her into making up. Eventually the two adults would grudgingly make up so the girls "wouldn't worry." By agreeing to make up "for the children's sake," neither of them lost face by apologizing or admitting a mistake. And because Miriam and Helen were available to rescue them, they didn't need to contain their own anger, so they "let it all hang out."

As adults, Miriam and Helen remained convinced that their parents couldn't make it through an argument without them. The two sisters, although married with families of their own, still lived near their parents and visited every day. Their parents' fights had become more vicious over the years, but whenever the talk of divorce became too real, their father threatened to commit suicide.

Both sisters had been anxious children and now were anxious adults. Helen's husband was a periodic drinker, and so Helen continued her role as rescuer and caretaker. Miriam's husband was moody and prone to depression; she was constantly trying to do as much as she could to "make life easier for Stan." Both women felt responsible for the moods of everyone around them and never expressed any needs of their own.

In therapy Miriam described her parents' ongoing battles and told me several times how she and her sister were best friends and could count on each other in any crisis.

"What crisis?" I finally asked Miriam. "Not yours surely, or your sister's, because you never share your own lives with each other."

Miriam looked surprised and a bit annoyed. "We don't need to," she said.

"Why not?"

"I wouldn't burden my sister with my troubles. She has enough of her own."

Like many caretakers and rescuers, she and Helen had been so burned out by their parents' needs that they considered being left alone an act of love and understanding.

"You and Helen think you're giving each other a gift by not burdening each other," I said. "But in fact you're closed off to each other. You only have enough to give to your parents, your spouses, or your children. You deserve more for yourselves."

Deserving something for herself was a new concept for Miriam. As she came to understand how her family functioned, she began working on responding differently to her parents' conflicts, with the long-term goal of being able to extricate herself entirely. She stopped visiting every day, told her parents that she enjoyed her visits much more when they were getting along, and slowly worked her way up to walking away from them when they began to fight.

The more Miriam changed, the more Helen tried to drag her back into the family fray. When Miriam held her ground, Helen became frantic with worry. This made Miriam anxious because she was loath to upset her sister. As the two sisters' compatible relationship went into a disruptive phase, the change became extremely uncomfortable for both of them. I reassured Miriam that this disruptive phase is almost impossible to avoid because siblings rarely change simultaneously. Miriam agreed that she had no choice but to continue her process of change.

Helen tried to continue her own role and fill in for Miriam, but could not. Finally she had to pull away. Her parents' conflicts escalated and then, miracle of miracles, subsided. Eventually they stopped fighting when their daughters were around.

This is not an uncommon resolution when siblings back out of parental conflicts. Without their children as a buffer, parents have to confront their own problems. Miriam's parents resolved theirs to the point where they didn't feel the need to involve their children.

Over time Miriam and Helen became much closer. They discovered that not only did they not want to burden each other with their problems, but they had rarely shared the really good things that happened to them either, for fear of engendering competitive feelings. Where once they had worried incessantly about how their mother and father were faring, now Miriam talked about what kind of work she wanted to pursue when her youngest child entered school; Helen proudly described the award she received at a local art show. As time went on, they expressed surprise at how little they actually knew about each other, and they vowed to make up for the time they had lost in shoring up their parents.

In the process of working on their relationship, their other relationships changed as well. Miriam, her husband, and their children went through some difficult times as she began to assert her own needs. Her husband resisted initially, but eventually they hammered out a more equal, enjoyable relationship. In fact, by coping with his problems himself instead of relying on Miriam to cushion his world for him, her husband began to feel better about himself and his abilities to function effectively in the world and with his children.

Helen's husband was more determined to draw Helen back in to her role as rescuer. He became involved with another woman and escalated his drinking bouts. She held her ground, and they eventually divorced. Helen continues to work on her relationship with her children.

What You Can Do

If you mediated your parents' conflicts for them, as an adult one of the hardest things for you to do is to sit back and let your relationships happen. Your tendency has been to rush in and smooth over awkward moments, and you may have lost sight of your own needs in the process. Learning to recognize, talk about, and take care of your own feelings is the next healthy step for you and your sibling.

If you encounter resistance from your sibling, don't give in. Assure your brother that you love him, that you want a relationship with him, but that helping and focusing on your parents is no longer a healthy option for you. Ask him to tell you how he feels; empathize with him if he tells you he's angry or anxious. Let him know you understand, but that you're not going to change your mind. Just as you cannot rescue your parents, you cannot rescue your brother or sister.

If your sibling continues to get involved in your parents' conflicts, make arrangements to see or talk to him away from your parents. Talk about your work, your kids, anything but your parents. In time you may find that this sharing feels natural to both of you and not something you have to strain to do. Then you are on your way to knowing each other and finally being able to have your own relationship.

Sometimes when siblings remove themselves from parental conflict, a parental split does occur, and you must be prepared for that possibility. Remember that if your parents choose to separate, *it will not be your fault*. In fact, if a breakup is in the cards, your "help" is just postponing the inevitable. All the same, if you and your sibling are accustomed to taking responsibility for your parents' well-being, this will be a very difficult time for you. Seeing your parents suffer has always been your cue to act. To protect yourselves, keep talking to each other about the process and about *your* feelings about what's going on in your family.

"She Should Help Take Care of Mother": Looking for Change for All the Wrong Reasons

Miriam was lucky that Helen saw as quickly as she did that the two of them needed to pull back from their parents' conflicts. Not all caretakers shift their allegiance from their parents to their sibling quite so readily. It took years of intense therapy for one of my clients, Fred, to extricate himself from a pathologically toxic family. Fred's parents were alcoholic and he and his brother, Clancy, had spent their childhood ricocheting from one parental crisis to another. As an adult Fred became determined to lead his own life, but Clancy continued to be enmeshed with their manipulative, abusive parents. He fought with Fred continually, begging him to come back into the fold. When Fred broke off all contact with his parents, Clancy could not accept his brother's flight into health and saw him as a traitor. Fred had no choice but to break off contact with Clancy as well.

Of course, not all sibling relationships blow up the way Fred and Clancy's did, but to one degree or another, the sibling who is left behind feels betrayed and usually tries to pull the other sibling back into the family conflicts. My client Ellen was left behind in her sister's flight to health, and Ellen was determined not to let her go.

Ellen first came to see me in therapy so that I could help her "make" her sister, Patricia, be more sensitive to their "poor mother." Their father had walked out on the family when Ellen was 11 and Patricia was 13. Ellen was furious about Patricia's "selfishness" and "complete lack of love and compassion." It was clear to me from our first session that Ellen was chained to her mother, who was depressed, self-pitying, and manipulative. Ellen had given up her own life to cook for, clean for, listen to, and endlessly sympathize with her mother, and until recently, so had her sister.

But now Patricia had moved to Denver. Their mother carried on to Ellen about how awful it was that Patricia had abandoned her, and Ellen spent hours on the telephone trying to talk Patricia into coming back home.

In telling me about these events, Ellen could barely speak; her hands trembled, and she burst into tears and repeatedly tore at her fingernails. "Patricia says horrible things about Mother bleeding her dry," she said, shaking her head violently.

Ellen was so involved with her mother that she couldn't understand why Patricia needed to leave, and she felt abandoned and angry. Unless Patricia came back and took up her old role, Ellen told me, she couldn't see any way to ever have a relationship with her again. Over the next few months, under the relentless pressure of both her mother and sister, Patricia stopped calling altogether, and the two sisters lost contact.

In therapy, Ellen and I focused on her relationship with her mother. I repeatedly pointed out her mother's complete lack of interest in her daughters' lives. With great difficulty Ellen learned to say no to her mother and to tolerate the fear that her mother would kill herself and it would be Ellen's fault. She moved into her own apartment and began dating someone seriously for the first time. Each time she made some progress in separating further from her mother, her mother would threaten suicide. But Ellen kept growing more self-aware, and each time she didn't cave in to her mother, she got stronger.

The more Ellen separated from her mother, the more she missed her sister. She wrote Patricia a letter saying she understood now that cutting off contact was the only way Patricia could get away from the problems in the family. She also told Patricia she would like to start up their relationship again.

Patricia responded immediately and was delighted at Ellen's remarks. They began corresponding, and Ellen made plans to visit her in Denver. When Ellen told her mother where she was going, her mother started to cry. For the next week, Ellen visited her mother every day, and every day found her sitting in the dark with a blanket around her shoulders.

Out of desperation, Ellen hatched a plan to surprise her mother by buying a ticket for her to visit Patricia as well. But when she called Patricia and told her about this plan, Patricia went into a rage. She said that Ellen had never cared about her or a relationship with her, and hung up.

Ellen canceled her flight, and when I met with her, she was hysterical and panicky. We talked through the events of the past week. I pointed out that Patricia and her father had not abandoned her mother but had been driven away by the woman's relentless, self-pitying manipulations. It took several sessions for Ellen to get her focus again. When she stopped identifying with her mother's pain, she saw how her mother had attempted to destroy her daughters' chances of having a relationship again.

Two months later, Ellen boarded a plane for Denver and showed up on her sister's doorstep. Patricia was shocked, but before she could say anything, Ellen said, "I'm sorry. I'm not here as an emissary for Mother, I'm here as your sister, and this time it's for real. I miss you."

The two sisters had a wonderful weekend together—free, for the first time, of the burden of taking care of their mother.

Changing Your Relationship

When I see people in therapy, I am alert to such remarks as "I want my sister to be good" or "I want my brother to be more sensitive to our father." Statements like these are the caretaker's hallmark. Try to be aware of caretaking comments yourself, both in speaking with and listening to your sibling.

If you are still involved with a parent's (or both parents') conflicts, then it is you who has to reevaluate your part. When your sibling tells you her feelings about removing herself from your unhealthy family system, try to really listen to her. If you feel angry or anxious, let her know. Take time to think about what your sibling has said. Evaluate your relationship with your parent and what role you are playing in your family. Concentrate on what needs *you* have that are being met. If you are solely concentrating on helping your parent, it is time for you to pull away.

If you have been working on releasing yourself from an unhealthy family system, your brother or sister may have already exerted pressure on you to change back to the role you played before. This is a good opportunity for you to talk to your sibling about why you've sought distance from the family and to encourage her to see you as a whole person, not as a cog in the family's machinery. Your sibling won't hear you if she's not ready. Probably the best way to make her come around is not to push, but to stay firm about what's best for you.

Disruptive Roles

If you mediated conflicts between your parents or took one parent's side over the other's, you probably did so in response to conflicts that were out in the open. There was nothing mysterious about the role you played—when your parents began to argue or your mother began to sink into depression, you stepped in to solve the problem as well as any child could be expected to. Today you probably know full well what role you have played in your family since childhood, painful as it may be to extricate yourself from it now.

It's much more difficult for adults who deflected their parents' conflicts as children to look back and understand exactly the role they played. To distract your parents, you and your siblings may have begun to fight every time the tension rose between them. Instead of dealing with their relationship, your parents may have turned their attention to you and your siblings and blamed you for bad behavior, abandoning, for the moment, their own conflicts. To this day it may be hard for you to see that your misbehavior was in fact a desperate bid to rescue your parents.

Parents who rope their kids into such a role are usually uncomfortable with conflict and don't know how to cope with angry feelings. Rather than letting their feelings "all hang out" and depending on their kids to glue their relationship back together, as Miriam and Helen's parents did, these parents rely on their children to deflect their anger before it gets to the boiling point.

The problem for such children when they reach adulthood is that they have trouble recognizing their own feelings; instead, they react to the tone of what's going on around them. For instance, you might intuitively pick up other people's tensions and react to them by changing the subject or telling jokes instead of finding out what the tension is about.

Sometimes, deflecting behavior can result in a compatible relationship with a sibling. For instance, when the parents of Elaine and Maggie started subtly digging at each other, the girls would launch into a comedy routine. They would trade one-liners, race around like the Marx Brothers making faces, and poke at each other, escalating the hysteria until their parents felt obliged to make them simmer down. As adults, these two sisters still become hyper and hysterical whenever they are together. Because their friends and co-workers tend to find their behavior embarrassing, Maggie and Elaine cling to each other even more. Although these roles are compatible at home with their parents—the two women are united in the same activity and not at odds with each other—they are not healthy or useful in the outside world.

Deflecting parental conflict doesn't always bring siblings closer together. More often it drives them apart, because most deflecting behavior is by nature contentious. For instance, Dolly's brother got their parents to stop fighting by hitting her and calling her names. As adults she still saw him as a troublemaker because he teased her relentlessly and poked fun at her kids.

Debbie's sister, Heather, climbed on their father's lap to get him to stop making cruel jokes about their mother's weight and housekeeping. As an adult, Debbie hates her sister because she is still "Daddy's little girl" and seductive with everybody, including Debbie's husband.

The most extreme, pathological version of a deflector is a child who acts out his parents' unexpressed (often completely denied) anger by being a troublemaker at home and perhaps a bully, truant, or drug user at school. By his wrongdoing he becomes the focus of his parents' attention. Parents of such children are often hand-wringers, presenting to school officials and others in the outside world a picture of confusion as to why their child is so "troubled." They frequently say things like, "We have such a happy family." As the family scapegoat, this targeted child is blamed—and may blame himself—for everything wrong in the family.

Because deflecting behaviors are unconscious, children easily take ownership of them. Dolly's brother didn't sit down and explain to himself that what he was doing when he hit her was "deflecting conflict," nor did Heather when she sat on her father's lap. Adult siblings may find it difficult to see that they each developed a specific role in response to parental tension, in large part because that tension was never acknowledged. Instead, they believe they didn't get along with their sibling because the brother or sister was always mean to them or poked fun at them. Margo and her two siblings are a prime example of how this sort of situation evolves.

"Margo's a Troublemaker": When Siblings Deflect Parental Conflict

When Margo entered therapy, she had no intention of or interest in delving into her relationship with her parents or siblings. Her problems, she told me, were "here and now." She was involved in one relationship after another, and every one of them ended in an explosive goodbye. When I asked what happened, she said she had no idea.

It quickly became clear that Margo couldn't express her anger over even the smallest things and didn't know how to discuss problems directly. For instance, if her boyfriend showed up late, she wouldn't express her anger at the time but instead would pick a fight later, flirt with somebody else, or suddenly become cold and distant later in the evening. It was difficult for Margo to explain her behavior, because most of the time she was not aware of her own anger.

She also couldn't tolerate her boyfriend's attempts to discuss specific problems in the relationship. If he wanted to make love and she didn't, or if he didn't like one of her friends, she would try to distract him from the problem at hand, change the subject, or get angry about something trivial. With so many pent-up feelings between them, eventually one of them would explode. When that happened Margo always assumed the relationship was over.

When I convinced Margo that relationship problems like the ones she was experiencing almost always have their origins in childhood, she began—reluctantly at first—to tell me about her background. Not surprisingly, we discovered that she had learned from her parents to avoid anger. Margo's mother and father argued often, but always over small things: who left the screen door open or why there wasn't any milk in the refrigerator. Both her parents were afraid to talk about feelings and to confront real problems in the relationship, so their anger came out in these other, roundabout ways. For example, Margo's father rarely offered to help with any household chores, even though both parents worked full-time outside of the home, but her mother never confronted him about it. Instead, when her husband sat down at the table expecting dinner, she slammed pots and pans around in the kitchen.

This was Margo's cue. Suddenly she would spill her milk, start to cry, and spit out her food. Both parents would turn their attention to her and become distracted by Margo's "sloppiness" or "willfullness." The tension between the parents would dissipate, Margo would calm down, and the family would finish their meal in peace.

Margo literally had been trained by her parents to behave as she did. Who knows how it first started? Perhaps she accidentally spilled her milk one day and her parents leaped on the opportunity to focus on something other than the tension between them, and Margo felt the difference. Maybe the next time they were tense with each other Margo threw her food on the floor. Soon, the habit was ingrained.

When her brother, Brett, was born, Margo added him to her repertoire; she kicked him, spat food on him, and pulled his hair. When her sister, Melanie, was born, Margo picked on her likewise, while Brett tried to defend the baby. Many mealtimes ended with all three children screaming. Their parents would jump into the sibling conflict and bypass their own.

Often, as in Margo's case, the oldest child establishes the pattern of how the parents' anger will be diverted. The ways in which the younger siblings are pulled into the pattern define the sibling relationships. Because Margo's diversionary tactics were disruptive to their relationship,

Brett and Melanie grew up seeing Margo as a troublemaker and a pushy older sister.

As adults Brett and Melanie were good friends and lived close by each other in Detroit. Margo had moved to California when she was in her twenties and went home only for the holidays. At family functions, the old dynamic would emerge. Though Margo no longer pulled hair or threw food, now she brought up political issues that infuriated Brett or Melanie. The name-calling would follow: Brett was a "sexist pig," Melanie a "political zero," and Margo, in turn, was a "bleeding heart."

As Margo explored her relationship with her parents in therapy, she began to see her relationship with her brother and sister in a different light. One day she said, "It was like a bell would go off and we would start going at each other. It never dawned on me that we went bonkers only when the folks were tense."

The next time she went home for the Christmas holidays, Margo made a real effort to change her behavior. She went out of her way to be nice to Melanie and Brett, who stuck together and watched her suspiciously. When her parents accused each other of having left the Christmas lights on the night before, Margo tensed up but didn't respond. To Margo's surprise, Brett stepped in and made a joke, and Melanie followed with another. The two younger siblings kept up their bantering until their parents joined in. Discovering that her two siblings had a way of their own of distracting their parents gave Margo the courage she needed to talk to them the next day.

She met with Melanie and Brett at a local diner to talk about how all of them had reacted to the tension between their parents. She mentioned her efforts to stay out of the fray the day before. Melanie looked at her skeptically, but Brett grew excited because he understood what she was talking about. "I have a few great memories of the two of us doing fun things together," Brett told Margo, "but only when we were outside the house, away from Mom and Dad. Somehow being around them prevented us from having a real relationship."

Melanie remained threatened by the new alliance between Margo and Brett for several months, but once she saw that Brett meant to stay her good friend, she softened. The three siblings continue to talk to one another by phone and through letters. Margo now looks forward to her family visits and to spending time with her siblings away from their parents. Their parents changed tactics and briefly tried to get their kids involved by complaining about each other; when that didn't work, they had a few big fights. The conflict frightened both of them, and they entered counseling together.

What You Can Do

The deflector role requires you to be something of a detective when it comes to your behavior or your sibling's. Looking at your current knee-jerk reactions to tense situations will help you to discover what kinds of behaviors you and your sibling were called upon to perform in order to defuse parental tension at home.

Look for signs in your own life of having deflected your parents' anger. If you and your sibling have a pattern of picking at each other, name-calling, or other distracting behavior, pay attention to how you react around others, especially your parents. If you sense tension and want to deflect it, resist your initial impulse. For instance, if you feel compelled to make a joke when your mother starts giving your father the silent treatment, don't do it. *You* stay silent instead. The tension will get worse, but before long, your parents will be reacting to each other differently. And, if not, assume they are comfortable with whatever tension there is between them.

Notice how you work out problems in your other relationships; often the habits you learned at home are transferred into your adult relationships as well. Do you laugh or make jokes to break the ice when you sense tension in others? Do you divert your own angry feelings because you haven't learned how to express them?

Be sure to pay attention to what your body is telling you. If you have frequent stomachaches, headaches, or a stiff neck, or if you grind your teeth at night, you may be reacting to tension in the people around you or in your relationships. Figure out when the tension started and try to get to the bottom of it. If your partner has a complaint or wants to talk about a particular feeling, listen to what she has to say. If you're angry yourself, say something about it. Admitting you're angry because your partner was late is better than pretending you're not angry and then ignoring her all night long.

"He's Just Like My Father, Selfish and Insensitive": When Siblings Take Opposite Sides in Parental Wars

If your parents' conflicts centered around a problem such as alcoholism, drug abuse, or violence toward one partner, you and your sibling probably sided with the parent who appeared to be the victim. Taking sides can also occur when one parent is manipulative and destructive, as in the case of Ellen and Patricia. In these instances your relationship with your sibling was probably compatible and you may seem to be close because you sided with the same parent. But in fact, you may know little about each other because you were focused on your parent's needs rather than your own.

A disruptive sibling relationship, in contrast, occurs when parents encourage their children to take sides by fighting their battles through their children. When parents are going through a divorce or feel powerless in their spousal relationship, both may manipulate the children into taking sides against the other parent. Sometimes parents stay involved in a hateful spousal relationship and use their children as cannon fodder in their wars with each other. When siblings side with different parents under these circumstances, their relationship is usually strained and defensive, even hateful and vicious.

If you sided with one parent over the other, chances are that as an adult you have difficulty in relating to people similar to the parent you sided against. You may find yourself taking sides with your friends or co-workers, getting involved in office politics, and siding with one of your kids over another. Because you have not been taught appropriate boundaries, you will interfere in other relationships—jumping in, for instance, to defend a friend in an argument that doesn't involve you.

When I saw my client Denise in therapy, she wanted to work on improving her relationships. Whenever she got involved in a serious relationship with a man, her mistrust surfaced and she constantly looked for signs of infidelity or signals that he was getting ready to leave her. If her boyfriend expressed any feelings that indicated to Denise that he was "wavering," she reacted by becoming angry and rejecting him. "I always leave first," she said, rather proudly.

She was opinionated and saw the world in black-and-white terms; one was either right or wrong. She was having problems in other relationships as well, because people saw her as rigid and unsympathetic. If Denise was on your side, however, she was a tremendous ally; loyal and willing to stick her neck out. As we talked about her history, it became clear that her mistrust and rigidity began when she and her older brother, Ted, took opposite sides in their parents' battles.

When Denise's parents divorced, she was 5 and Ted was 10. Their parents' fighting had intensified into violence more than once, and by the time they divorced, they could not be in the same room without screaming accusations and obscenities at each other. At some point during their arguments, Denise's mother would swoop her up, carry her into the bedroom, slam the door, and then hold on to Denise and sob. Ted and his father would then leave the house and come back a few hours later, usually with some new toy for Ted.

After the divorce, Denise's mother would take Denise to the park on Saturday mornings. By the time they returned to the house, Denise's father had picked up Ted to go ice-skating, miniature golfing, or fishing. The few times that Denise was still home when her father arrived, he would explain that she was too young to go with him and Ted, and that when she got older she could tag along. Denise was hurt and confused by her father's disinterest in her. On top of it all, Ted would come home and tell her about the fun things he had done that day with his father. Ted, of course, thought his father was the greatest.

When her mother saw how hurt Denise was, she explained that her father was insensitive and that was why she had divorced him in the first place. Soon, when Ted talked about how great their dad was, Denise replied that Dad wasn't great at all and was, in fact, an insensitive jerk. Then Ted would say, "You sound just like Mom. That's why Dad left in the first place, because she drove him away." Before long, she and Ted were screaming at each other, each one defending one parent.

When I saw Denise in therapy, she was in her mid-thirties and still extremely close to her mother. She had almost no contact with her father or Ted. For several months we focused on her angry and hurt feelings at her father for abandoning her. She began to see how her father's betrayal had led to her feelings of mistrust in her current relationships with men.

I questioned her some time later about Ted, but she dismissed him as "just like my father, selfish and insensitive." I expressed concern that she and Ted had been caught up in their parents' rancorous divorce and had been unfairly used by both parents. This was a novel idea to Denise. At first she defended her mother fiercely. Once the seed was planted, however, she began noticing how quick her mother was to criticize not just her ex-husband, but Ted as well. One day Denise said to me, "My parents each chose one of us and squared off, and they never even gave a thought to Ted or me."

She contacted Ted and invited him to join her for coffee. When they met, Denise asked him about his wife and two kids. He looked at her suspiciously but answered, and she was surprised to hear how sweetly he described his new baby girl. She then told him what she had been working on, and he seemed to listen with interest and curiosity. When she mentioned how she had sided with their mother and he with their father, he instantly began criticizing their mother for treating their father badly during the divorce.

"That's exactly what I'm talking about, Ted," Denise told him. "We've always jumped on their bandwagon. You've been on Dad's and I've been on Mother's. They've been divorced over 20 years by now, they never see each other, and here we are arguing about their marriage."

"Well, if Mother had been a little kinder they never would have got divorced in the first place."

"Well, who left who?" Denise shouted, and before she knew it, she and Ted were acting like they always had, each defending one parent and not even discussing themselves. "This is pointless," Denise said finally and stormed out of the restaurant.

To her surprise Ted called her that night. "You're right," he said. "I don't know a thing about you, except I've assumed you're just like Mom."

As Denise told me later, she had to stifle her initial reaction, which was to say, "Well, what's wrong with that? It's better than being like Dad!"

She and Ted agreed to get together again, and when they did, they decided that for the time being they would not even mention their parents. They gave themselves a chance to get to know each other. They spent their time together asking and answering questions and finding out who they each were.

Changing Your Relationship

If you and your sibling sat on different sides of the parental fence, you, too, probably have a lot of negative feelings toward each other. The biggest and most necessary step you will have to take is to begin separating your sibling from your parent. Don't assume that your brother is just like your father, or that your sister is the spitting image of your mother.

Tell your sibling you want to get to know *him*. Explain that because you have been on opposite sides of a war you never started, neither of you has had an opportunity to get to know the other. Stop defending *your* parent. If your brother goes on about how wonderful or mistreated *his* parent is, stop him and tell him you are more interested in hearing about him. Ask questions about your brother. Find out who he is. Tell him about yourself.

After talking for a while, bring up the fact that both of you were treated unfairly and used by your parents. If your sibling finds this too painful, be sensitive to his feelings, and don't pursue the subject if your sibling doesn't want to. Instead, focus on how you can both improve your relationship in the future.

As you can see from these examples, it is not the roles per se that you and your sibling took on, but how they worked or didn't work together that determined what your relationship with your sibling is now. Whether these roles were compatible or disruptive, they have caused you problems in your sibling relationships and with your other relationships in the present.

Releasing yourself from the restrictions of these roles and removing yourself from the parental vise is essential to your growth as a person and your improved relationship with your sibling.

CHAPTER EIGHT

"I've Never Been Able to Stand Up to Him"

Coming to Terms with Violence and Neglect

When parents abuse children physically or emotionally, by hitting, slapping, or taunting them, they teach their sons and daughters an absolute lack of respect for their own body and spirit. The same is true when parents neglect children by ignoring them, failing to feed them, or leaving them alone when they are too young to take care of themselves. Parental neglect and abuse severely damage children's self-esteem and their ability to love, trust, or be loved.

Most abused or neglected children believe they have done something to deserve their parents' wrath or neglect. If your parents abused or neglected you, you probably grew up believing that if you tried harder or did the right thing, your parents would then love you and treat you properly. Of course, nothing you did made any difference, as your parents' anger was inside of them and would have come out no matter what. Your parents were probably victims of abuse or neglect themselves, or were strung out on drugs, and did not know how to nurture children.

Siblings from homes such as these often treat each other the same way their parents treat them. Sibling abuse runs the gamut from name-calling, slapping, putdowns, and taunting, to beating, sexual abuse, and mental cruelty. If your mother slapped you when you cried, ignored you when you were hungry, laughed at you when you made a mistake, you probably did those same things to your younger siblings when the rage you felt at your mother became too much to bear. Similarly, if your father slammed your older brother up against the wall for no apparent reason, there's a good chance your brother took out his rage on you when your father wasn't around. If you grew up in a home where the slowest kid out of the room got beaten when Mom or Dad had a few too many, you learned to run fast in order to save yourself. Today your relationships with your brothers and sisters are probably filled with anger, feelings of abandonment and betrayal, and shame.

Growing up in a violent home, you may have learned that there are only two roles, victim and aggressor. All children start out as victims, but in order to stop feeling helpless, older siblings often eventually take on the role of the aggressor. They take out their pent-up rage and helplessness on their younger siblings. In this way violence climbs down the ladder, from oldest to youngest.

In some families older siblings discover another role, that of rescuer or protector. In these families, children often form strong attachments that last a lifetime, but the siblings pay a price. If you assumed the role of rescuer or protector, you never had the opportunity to show hurt or vulnerability. Instead, you grew up rapidly and became a parent to your younger sibling, a responsibility that no child is equipped to handle. If you were protected by an older brother or sister, you probably had inordinately high expectations of your protector, expecting him or her to be more perfect as a parent than any sibling could possibly be. And, because your relationship has been so unequal, you may never have developed confidence in your ability to take care of yourself. This lack of confidence has had an impact on every area of your life.

Sibling abuse is a more serious problem then most of us recognize, especially since neighbors, teachers, parents, and even law enforcement officials often dismiss physical abuse of one sibling by another as "part of growing up." My client Bill's third-grade teacher, for instance, was concerned when she noticed bruises on his arms and face. When he told her that his older brother regularly beat him up, she shook her head, smiled, and said, "Oh, you boys are so rough on each other." Bill protested that in fact he couldn't fight back because his brother was five years older and much bigger than he was. "You'll have to try harder not to tease your brother or provoke him," she responded. Bill's brother continued to beat him almost every day until he moved out of the house when Bill was 13.

If you were victimized by a parent or older sibling, you may be repeating that role in your current relationships, perhaps by marrying an abuser or working for an abusive boss. Because of your fear and vulnerability, you are a prime target for abusive people. If you physically or verbally abused a sibling, there's a good chance that as an adult you're continuing that pattern with a spouse or your own child. Turning into an abuser has allowed you to feel more powerful than if you remained a victim. But underneath the abuser in you is a hurt child, a child you don't want to uncover because you don't know how to protect him other than by hitting first.

Now, as a victimized or abusive adult, you may want to work on salvaging your sibling relationship as part of turning all the relationships in your life around. On the other hand, your relationship with your sibling may be so powerfully destructive that you need help, not in mending the relationship, but in ending it. The anecdotes that follow illustrate both alternatives. I hope they will help you decide what is best for you.

"I Don't Trust Anybody, My Brothers Included": The Erosion of Trust in a Violent Home

Parents who cannot contain their rage spill it out at inappropriate times. They beat their children, not as punishment for a specific wrongdoing, but simply to vent their anger. Their children live on constantly shifting ground, never knowing when something will set their parents off.

A child in such an environment has no idea why she is being punished at any given time. Because there is no rhyme or reason to the way her parents react to her, she never learns to trust herself or others, or to make sense of her world. Instead, she spends an inordinate amount of time monitoring those around her, looking for signs to explain why she has angered them yet again.

Children in such families live in fear of unpredictable violence, and their main goal is to stay out of the way when their parent gets angry. Often a parent's rage is not directed at a particular child but at whoever happens to be in the room. Siblings thus get into the habit of escaping when they sense a parent's building rage. As my client Rick said about himself and his brothers, "It was every boy for himself. The last one out of the room was the one Dad grabbed. So we learned to run, and run fast."

As adults, Rick and his brothers shared a sense of humor about their childhood and had a million stories of abuse to tell, all with a funny twist. But underneath the laughter were anger and sadness. Now in their forties and fifties, these men wanted more than anything to like one another, but they were held back by the knowledge that when push came to shove, each would scramble for the door, every man for himself.

Rick came into therapy because he was having difficulties at work. When he made a mistake he was quick to blame other people, and as his boss put it, "Something goes wrong and you're nowhere to be found."

When Rick repeated his supervisor's remark, he laughed. "I grew up running," he said. "I'm going to have to learn how to stand still." Then he became serious for a moment. "I'm also here because I'm not sure I can really love my two-year-old son, Greg." Rick described how his temper was set off when his son spit out food or pushed a toy away. "I have such a short fuse," Rick said. "When I get angry at Greg I try to leave the room, but sometimes I don't leave in time and I scream at him or shake him." Now Rick and his wife were expecting a second child, and Rick was afraid he would someday explode with the anger he felt inside.

As we talked about his history, Rick understood clearly that he had inherited his anger and his urge to take it out on Greg. Rick's father had broken rakes over Rick's head, snapped his wrist until it broke, and punched him until he was black and blue on every part of his body. His two brothers, one older, one younger, had received the same treatment.

I asked about Rick's relationship with his brothers now. "We get together, talk about the old times some, hang out, have a few beers," he said. "We don't have much to say to each other. Men don't sit around and talk like you women do," he added.

As I got to know Rick, I saw a different picture of how the brothers' visits unfolded. They would get together on a Sunday to watch a football or basketball game. One of them would begin to reminisce about the time their father beat Rick with the rake, or the time he chased Tom out into the pasture and beat him "within an inch of his life" with the butt of his shotgun and the steel toes of his boots. All three brothers would laugh as if this was the funniest thing they had ever heard and then joke about several other beatings they had received as boys. But inevitably their feelings of camaraderie would fade, and one or the other of them would change the subject. By telling and retelling their stories, the three brothers were trying to purge themselves of their awful memories. But they always got stuck at the same spots, because they never talked about how each of them felt abandoned by the others and cowardly himself for trying to get out of their father's way.

I did my best to assure Rick that he and his brothers had done nothing wrong. I then urged him to talk about the emotions that none of the brothers ever mentioned, the feelings of guilt and shame.

The next time he and his brothers got together, Rick did just that. He told his younger brother, Jim, that he had sometimes felt ashamed for running away. Jim stopped mid-sentence, stunned. He took a big gulp of beer and looked back at the TV set.

Rick's older brother, Tom, said quietly, as they all faced the TV, "I felt that way about both you guys. I was the oldest and I should have protected you."

For the next several hours the men talked about their childhood without making light of it. They turned off the TV, moved to the kitchen table, and forgot about dinner.

At some point Rick said, "The worst part for me now is remembering those times when I pointed the finger at one of you, even if something was my fault. I was such a coward. And I do the same thing at work. I'll do anything to avoid getting into trouble."

Jim looked at him and kind of laughed. "Me too. What a sorry bunch we are."

Rick made a special effort to understand and control his violent impulses toward his son, Greg. It wasn't easy, as his responses to the child were immediate, unprovoked, and overwhelming. His younger brother, Jim, experienced the same problems with his children, and the two men found they could talk to each other about their anger and offer support.

Unfortunately, Rick's older brother, Tom, didn't recognize his behavior toward his two boys as abuse. He justified his yelling and hitting by insisting that, unlike his father, he always hit his sons for a reason, "not just because I feel like it."

Their father still worked the family farm, and occasionally Rick and Jim would drive out to lend a hand. Their father never thanked his sons for helping, often criticized their work, and addressed each of them as "Hey you." Rick told me he was so accustomed to the abuse that he "tuned it out." Their father had long since stopped hitting them; as Rick said, "He can't move fast enough."

One weekend at the farm, Rick overheard his father yelling at Greg, "Hey you, move your ass out of the way." Rick ran over to Greg, picked him up, and screamed at his father, "Don't you talk like that to my son again!"

Before he knew it, Rick was crying. "I just kept holding on to my boy and screaming at my father, telling him to never, never hurt my son," he told me. Jim came running over and hugged Rick. "That was the first time my brother and I had ever touched each other, except by accident," Rick said. Rick's father had stared at his sons for a moment and then walked quickly away.

Once Rick stood up to his father, he felt a tremendous freedom. Each time he saw his father after that, Rick refused to take any abuse from him. He continued to work on controlling his angry impulses. As time went on, this became easier as the explosive anger he had always felt inside drained away. By confronting the source of his own anger, Rick was beginning to heal himself.

What You Can Do

Growing up in an abusive family has taught you certain ways of surviving. It's important that you and your siblings don't blame yourselves or each other for trying to escape a parent's wrath. It's normal for abused children to blame their siblings to avoid a beating, to try to be the first one out of the room, or to hope their sibling gets a beating instead of them. However, these same responses will seriously impede your ability to trust and have healthy relationships as an adult. Your reactions as a child were situationally appropriate, but now the trick is to learn that not all situations in life mimic the household in which you grew up.

Don't be surprised if it takes you a long time to trust that others won't react abusively to you. It took Rick months to be able to change his behavior at work. He found himself standing in his boss's office shaking from head to toe, waiting to be "beaten" for having made a clerical error. Eventually he found that he could tolerate the anxiety because he saw that his boss did not want to punish him but simply needed to know what could be done to correct the error.

Learn ways to control your own impulse to strike out. Counting to 10 and leaving the room are good behaviors to have in your repertoire. Recognize signs in yourself of distress or stress—a fast pulse, a short fuse, nervous energy, a feeling that you need to blow off some steam. When you feel this way, go into a room, close the door, and punch a pillow, scream, kick your mattress. Pound your fist into a pillow or mattress until you are exhausted. Express your feelings *before* they get to the boiling point. Most adults who were abused as children were never allowed to express any feelings of their own. This buildup of anger is toxic to you and dangerous to the people you love. Take action to dissipate this anger safely as often as you need to.

Talking to your sibling about your efforts may be a bridge to closeness for both of you. By addressing your feelings, you are opening up the possibilities of discussing your childhood in ways that you probably have not done before.

"He Was as Bad as My Stepfather": When Parental Abuse Triggers Sibling Abuse

When children are abused by a parent, they often mimic that behavior with younger siblings. Powerless over their parents, they have a sense of control over their younger siblings, who also provide a convenient outlet for their feelings of rage and helplessness. When an older sibling establishes an abusive role with a younger sibling, the abuse often continues into adulthood unless one of them makes a concerted effort to change. The abuse may shift from physical to verbal attack or otherwise become more subtle and "grownup," but the feelings it evokes remain the same.

This was the case for Dolores, who entered therapy because she felt stymied at work. She was timid, unsure of herself, and easily persuaded that she had made a mistake when she hadn't. As a result, she was reluctant to share new ideas for fear of being ridiculed, and she had been stuck at the same job for four years. She was also subject to severe bouts of depression in which she would be consumed by feelings of self-hatred.

When they were kids, Dolores' brother, Mel, four years her senior, had treated her the same way their stepfather treated him. He picked her up off the floor by her ears, dragged her across the room by her hair, slapped her, and once pushed her down the cellar stairs and broke her collarbone.

Just about the time that their stepfather stopped hitting him, Mel stopped hitting Dolores and shifted to verbal abuse and humiliation. Their mother never intervened, pretending that the abuse Mel heaped on his sister was normal sibling rivalry. Similarly, she excused the way her husband treated her kids by saying, "They're lucky he pays attention to them at all."

A few months after she began therapy, Dolores went back to Kansas City to visit her family. Mel was waiting as she stepped off the Jetway. "Lost a little more weight?" he asked, looking her up and down. "No wonder you're not married yet. Who wants a bag of bones?" During the course of the weekend he criticized her friends, her job, her apartment, none of which he had ever seen. By the time she left, she felt beaten down, stupid, and ugly.

Rationally, Dolores and I could dispute each of Mel's putdowns, but the history between them went beyond his words. The overall effect of his constant criticism had been devastating. In Mel's presence, Dolores became a child again beaten up by her brother. By now, their pattern was so set that Dolores reacted to his words as if they were physical blows: she became smaller and smaller.

After her visit home, Dolores slipped into a deep depression and told me she felt like a "piece of dirt." But after a few weeks of talking about it, she saw for the first time the connection between her depression and anger. She was angry at her brother, but she had never been able to express it, so she turned it upon herself. As she worked through her feelings about her brother, her other relationships came into focus, too. "I've made the world into my brother," she said. "I'm convinced everyone is going to treat me like he does, and I feel so defenseless, like a little kid."

Dolores had to learn two things: first, that everyone was not like her brother; and second, that she didn't have to cave in to her brother or anyone else. Once she took the time to look around her, she found people who didn't criticize everything she said or wore. She began to seek these people out and to open up around them. The effort was terrifying at first, but the positive reactions she received kept her going.

Dolores worked with a man given to verbal abuse, and we agreed that he presented a golden opportunity to change her way of dealing with people like Mel. Dolores learned to walk away from this co-worker's criticisms and not to take his words to heart. She also learned to disagree with him and to stand up for herself, even when he tried to undercut her by criticizing her work to their boss.

Eventually she learned to trust her assessment of other people. As an exercise I encouraged her to predict what she thought a person's reaction would be to her in any given situation. Once she saw that she was right most of the time, she began to trust her intuition. Of course, she couldn't accurately predict people's responses all the time. But gradually she learned to take chances and to accept negative or disinterested responses. As she became more outgoing and shared her ideas at work more readily, her employer sat up and took notice. Before long, she was promoted.

The next time Dolores visited Kansas City, Mel met her again at the airport. When he commented on her weight, she ignored him. When he pooh-poohed her promotion, she told him he hurt her feelings. Momentarily stunned, he quickly recovered and made fun of her "sensitivity." Taking a deep breath, Dolores told him that if he didn't have anything good to say to her, she would prefer to confine her visit to seeing her parents. "I didn't come all the way back home to be made fun of or criticized," she told him, her heart pounding.

Mel kept his distance over the weekend. When he started falling back into his old pattern, Dolores called him on it. When he drove her to the airport, he tried to criticize her for "playing up" to their mother, but his remarks fell flat. Soon they were riding in silence. Right before she hopped out, she told him that when he was ready, she wanted to talk to him about their childhood and the abuse he suffered at the hands of their stepfather. "I'd like us to have a healthier relationship one day," she said. Mel sat unmoving, watching her take her suitcase out of the back of the truck.

Dolores told me she doesn't care whether Mel takes her up on her offer to work on a better relationship. "I don't want to put my energy there," she said. "I want to concentrate on having healthy relationships. If he comes around, fine."

When Dolores freed herself from the confines of her relationship with Mel, a whole new world opened up to her. "I'm finally the person I was meant to be before I got sidetracked by a maladjusted family," she said to me. "Now I have radar for people like Mel. I stay away from them and don't let them come close to me."

Dolores also found that she had radar for detecting sensitive people like herself, and she began to go out of her way to bring them out of their shells. By being supportive and listening to them, she said, she was learning to heal herself.

Changing an Abusive Relationship

If you were abused by an older sibling as Dolores was, an important first step in healing is to avoid people like your sibling. Don't seek them out, don't tell them your ideas, don't open yourself up to criticism from them. Examine each area of your life: if you have a boss who abuses you, consider changing jobs; if your girlfriend is abusive, plan to separate. Up until now you have probably seen yourself as the problem. Learning to be inner-directed—in other words, to judge yourself on your own terms instead of letting others judge you on theirs—is essential to regaining your self-esteem. These are some ways you can build up your self esteem: Work as hard as you can at a chosen project, and congratulate yourself for a job well done. Constantly reinforce to yourself that you are a good person. Turn off your interior critical voice when you hear it.

When you feel strong enough, you may want to tell your sibling, like Dolores did, that you will no longer tolerate abusive behavior. *If your sibling is still physically abusive to you, or if saying something to him will incite him to abuse you now, do not confront him alone, or avoid him altogether. The reason to confront a sibling is for your benefit; if it won't help, don't do it.*

A safe way to confront an abusive sibling is to invite him to a therapy session or to another place where a trusted third party will be present. Another way is by writing him a letter.

If you decide you want to avoid your sibling, consider visiting your family at times when your sibling will not be present. Be prepared for your parents to be less than helpful, however. Since the abuse has always occurred under your parents' noses, there is not much reason to think they will admit the abuse now or help you cope with it. Don't let their indifference deter you. You have a right to tell them how you feel, what you expected from them in the past and didn't get, and what you expect from them now.

"Dinnertime at Our House Was Like Being Thrown to the Lions": When Parents Encourage Sibling Abuse

Children who grow up in an atmosphere of criticism, anger, or physical abuse become closed off and defensive or defiant. Not surprisingly, they refuse to show their vulnerability, either to their parents or siblings. Often parents vent their own cruelty by encouraging their children to react to their siblings with sarcasm and teasing, and reward them with attention when they "go for the jugular."

My client Anita and her five siblings grew up in a home with a critical, sadistic father and a passive, manipulative mother. When I met Anita, she was in her mid-thirties and still paying the price for her upbringing in every one of her relationships.

Anita sought counseling because her relationship with her husband was falling apart. They were trading insults and blame back and forth. On top of that, her employees had complained to her boss that she was too critical and demanding. She was angry about these developments and extremely defensive; she thought everyone else had a problem but her. "Of course I have high standards," she told me when we first met. "I expect a lot from people, but not any more than I expect from myself." What we discovered as we went along was not that Anita had impossibly high standards, but that she didn't know how to praise a job well done or to encourage others. All her comments to her husband and employees focused on what she perceived as their shortcomings.

When I asked about her childhood, she said that dinner with her parents and siblings had been "like being thrown to the lions." Every night her father would ask the children what they had done that day. Every night as they answered, he would rip them apart. "That's right, Anita, keep stuffing your face. Ted here's got lockjaw. Can't get his mouth to work to tell us why he got his ass kicked on the football field." If they got angry or—worse yet—broke down and cried, their father stepped up his criticism. The correct response was to laugh and criticize someone else in a caustically "funny" way. Anita's mother spent all her time running back and forth serving the food. Later she could be found eating her dinner, out of harm's way, in the kitchen while she did the dishes.

When Anita and her brothers and sisters got together as adults, they spent the whole time digging at one another. Anita was "Thunder Thighs," Alissa was "missing a major key," Brad was "Crater Face," and so on. Brad's wife had mentioned to one of the siblings that the couple's inability to have children was Brad's "fault." This information proved to be a constant source of amusement for everyone. For Christmas Anita gave Brad a sex manual, and his brother Ted gift-wrapped some of his own sperm in a cup. When I pointed out how cruel their behavior was, Anita shrugged and said coldly, "His wife should have kept her mouth shut, then. He's fair game now."

To drop the defense of sarcasm and cruelty was to risk being mutilated even further. "I don't know how to be any other way," Anita said . "That's the way I think, the way I feel inside."

In order to understand her impulse to strike out at people, Anita had to go back to her early childhood, to remember what it was like when she could still feel the sting of her father's cruelty. It was only after she could feel that hurt inside that she could sympathize with the same feelings in other people.

Anita had to build herself back up from scratch, a process that took several years. During that time, she went through a divorce and lost her job. She avoided her family because she felt unable to protect herself from their inevitable attacks and unable to express how she was feeling.

Anita wrote a letter to each of her siblings and to her parents vowing that she would never again sit down to dinner with her family as long as she and her siblings were "served up as the main course." Although her two older brothers called to tell her what a "crock" her letter was, her younger brother and two sisters offered to join the protest.

It's still hard work for Anita to be supportive of others; it simply doesn't come easily for her. But now she's capable of stopping herself mid-sentence when she catches herself criticizing her boyfriend. She often feels frustrated with her progress, but I keep reminding her that she has come a long way from the angry, defensive woman I first met.

What You Can Do

If you and your sibling have adopted an abusive, critical, taunting, caustic manner as a protection against vulnerability and hurt, it will be difficult to give it up. A good first step is to tell your sibling that you are going to stop criticizing or abusing her. If it is too frightening to say this sort of thing, let your actions speak for you.

Changing your relationship will require a strong will on your part. Chances are your sibling will try to pull you back into the usual pattern by abusing you even more. But instead of trying to think of a retort, let the comment sink in and allow your other feelings—like hurt—to surface. This is a painful but necessary step for you to take in order to begin to have more appropriate responses to cruel, hurtful comments. An added benefit is that if you can resist responding to your sibling's digs, eventually the abuse will stop.

If you fall back into your old abusive behavior with your sibling, apologize. This may stun your sibling, but your acknowledgment that you hurt her, even if she doesn't realize it, will slowly begin to change your relationship.

To change your other relationships, you need to become more sensitive to the way your flip remarks hurt other people's feelings. You may have to stop expressing your sense of humor altogether if the way you poke fun is not fun at all but cruel. Pay attention to others and be aware of caustic or hurtful remarks. Of course, you have been taught to tune out people's feelings, so it will be difficult for you in the beginning to become sensitive, but keep at it. Once you are on the alert for people's reactions to you, you will eventually be able to tell whether your humor is funny or hurtful. This will take time, but it's well worth the effort.

"How Can I Let Her Down?" The Co-Dependent Sibling

Sometimes children who are abused or neglected by their parents find comfort in each other. Rather than taking out their rage on each other, they form a strong bond that lasts into adulthood. But the bond that offered safe harbor in childhood may come to feel constricting in adulthood. This was true for my client Ruby and her sister, Bea.

Ruby came to see me because she was distraught over Bea's drug problems. She wanted me to help her get Bea to stop using cocaine. She was desperate and talked only of her sister's problems the whole first session. Whenever I tried to get her to talk about herself, she would become agitated and her body would tense up, waiting for me to finish so she could get back to her subject: her sister.

At the next session, I insisted that Ruby tell me something about her family, and she calmed down long enough to tell me the sad story of her childhood. Ruby was the youngest child of three. Bea was one year older and Ben five years older than Ruby. Their father was a heroin and cocaine addict, in and out of prison for most of Ruby's childhood. When he was in jail, Ruby's mother went out on the town, leaving the three children alone to fend for themselves. When her father was home, he beat Ruby's mother. He once stabbed her in the stomach, and threatened to kill her several times. Ben, too, was the target of their father's rage; he usually had bruises, cuts, or burns on some part of his body.

When their parents bothered to notice Ruby and Bea at all, usually they yelled at or hit them. Ben sometimes hit or kicked them too, but as they got older, the girls learned to stay out of his way. Neither of their parents brought food into the house on a regular basis or bothered to do laundry. Bea and Ruby took money from their mother's or father's pockets to buy food or to wash their clothes at the laundromat. They slept together, ate together, played together, and defended each other from other kids in the neighborhood.

"We wouldn't have made it out of there if we didn't have each other," Ruby told me. "Bea and I had a pact, growing up: we would always be there for each other, no matter what."

Their father died of a drug overdose when Ruby was 12. Following in his footsteps, Ben became a drug dealer when he was in his teens and was shot and killed when Ruby was 15.

Ruby was in her late twenties when I met her. She and Bea shared an apartment that Ruby paid for. Bea had dropped out of high school and had difficulty holding a job, whereas Ruby had managed to go to real estate school and was a successful commercial real estate agent. Several months earlier, Bea had started going out with a man whom Ruby didn't like. Ruby recognized him as one of her brother's old friends and suspected that he too was a drug dealer. When she confronted Bea, her sister angrily told her to "stay out of my life."

Over the last few months, Bea had begun disappearing, sometimes for days at a time. Eventually Ruby always found Bea in the old neighborhood, strung out on crack or heroin, sometimes dirty and belligerent, sometimes full of remorse. Ruby would bring her back to the apartment and help her to get straight. During this time, Bea would cry and apologize and promise never to use drugs again. Ruby would buy her new clothes or do something else nice for Bea to make her feel better. The two sisters would get close again, hang out together, and Ruby would feel hopeful that this time Bea was off drugs for good. Then Bea would disappear again.

Ruby begged me to help. "Poor Bea," she kept saying, "she can't help it, she doesn't have any control. She needs me, she'll die out there without me. I have to do something."

"You can't save your sister from drugs," I said. "And I can't help you save your sister from drugs. Only your sister can save herself from drugs. You have to let go, Ruby." Ruby bowed her head, in both relief and pain, and cried.

For several months Ruby and I worked on her separation from Bea. She went to meetings of Al-Anon, a group where family and friends of addicts and alcoholics gather for support and understanding. She also began attending CODA (Codependents Anonymous) meetings. However, throughout all these meetings and her sessions with me, she continued to rescue her sister whenever Bea disappeared.

About six months into our therapy, Bea disappeared again, and although Ruby searched for her, she couldn't find her. A year went by. During that year, Ruby went through hell. She felt betrayed, angry, hurt, scared. She wondered if she had tried hard enough, if she could have done something different and saved her sister. She constantly woke up from nightmares about getting a phone call telling her her sister was dead. I kept reminding her that Bea had made a choice. "She may be like your father and Ben, but remember that many addicts choose to stop being addicts."

One of the hardest things for Ruby to do was to let go of her sister and face her own feelings of aloneness and helplessness. She didn't trust other people, but she had never felt she had to, because she and her sister had each other. "Now, I don't have anyone and I don't know how to talk to people, get to know people or let them get to know me."

She finally got a phone call from Bea. She was in jail in San Francisco. Ruby was relieved. "At least I know she's not dead, and that she has a chance to get straight."

When Bea got out of jail, she and Ruby resumed their relationship. Just when Ruby began to trust her sister again, Bea disappeared for a weekend. This time, however, Ruby didn't look for her. By now, Ruby recognized that by trying to help Bea, she was really trying to help herself and to hold on to something that no longer existed. She wanted to will her sister into health because she couldn't bear to be alone and go through life without Bea. To fill the emptiness she felt, she became active in her church and accepted offers from co-workers to go out for dinner or drinks after work. While she was socializing she felt alone and even guilty for continuing with her life, but after a time she began to feel better.

"It's the hardest thing I've had to do in my life," Ruby said to me, "letting go of my sister, and still loving her."

Changing Your Relationship

If you find yourself in a situation similar to Ruby and Bea's, you will have to focus on what your relationship with your sibling is in the present, not what it was when you were kids. Mourn the loss of your relationship. Allow yourself to feel the pain of recognizing what your relationship is now, as opposed to what it used to be.

Let your sibling go. You cannot protect her from drug addiction, alcoholism, or other destructive behaviors. Your love alone is not enough. Your sibling has to make the choice to love herself. Your sibling must decide what to do with her life.

This isn't to say you can't be supportive. Tell your sibling that you love her but that you will no longer try to rescue her from herself. Don't loan her money, bail her out of jail, or make excuses for her. It's up to you to decide if you want to set limits on when you will see your sibling. For instance, Ruby told Bea that she wasn't willing to see Bea when she was high on drugs.

If your sibling asks you to go to an A.A. or C.A. meeting with her, by all means do so. Support her attempts at health, but don't take responsibility for her acts of self-destruction. Each of you has experienced pain in growing up, and you must realize that each of you has learned different methods of trying to cope with your pain. If your sibling seems bent on destroying herself, you can only hope that someday she will gain the strength to get help.

Concentrate on yourself by going to Al-Anon or CODA meetings, or, if appropriate, meetings of Adult Children of Alcoholics. While focusing on yourself, question your need to rescue. I've mentioned this problem in previous chapters because it's a frequent, unhealthy dynamic with many siblings. As the rescuer, you must recognize *your* part of the problem and work on resolving it. By rescuing your sibling you are trying to control a situation that you cannot *and should not* control. If you are engaged in co-dependent behavior with your sibling, you are doing the same in other relationships. You deserve to have healthier relationships, ones that reward you, that nourish you, that make you feel good about yourself and your contribution to a relationship.

Coming from an abusive home has left you and your sibling struggling to fight your own battles with abuse, self-worth, and trust. I hope that by working on your relationship with your sibling, whether it be ending an abusive relationship or coming closer to a sibling who also was abused, some of your wounds will begin to heal.

Unfortunately, not all abuse is physical or emotional. Many children are also subject to sexual abuse and incest, both from parents and siblings. I'll be discussing these problems in the next chapter.

CHAPTER NINE

"We Couldn't Talk About It"

Facing the Trauma of Sexual Abuse and Incest

Sexual abuse severely damages sibling relationships. Children who live in homes where sexual abuse is occurring do not talk to each other about it, rarely comfort each other, and frequently deny that any abuse is going on at all. If your father was molesting your sister, you may have felt relief that you were not his victim, guilty for not helping her, or shame for knowing the abuse was going on. If you were the one abused, you may have felt angry that your siblings couldn't help you, or shame that they knew what was going on and blamed you.

In response, sexually abused children numb themselves to their feelings. They don't make a connection between what they are doing now as adults—being sexually promiscuous, drinking, or taking drugs—with

171

what was done to them as children. Another response to childhood sexual trauma is that, as adults, you and your siblings are probably distant from one another, or may even avoid one another, because you don't know how to talk about what happened.

About one in every three women and one in every seven men are sexually abused by the time they are 18 years old. In many homes, it is not only parents or other adult relatives who are the abusers, but siblings who sexually abuse their brothers and sisters. Sibling abuse, both physical and sexual, is often dismissed or ignored, just as parental abuse was a few years ago, but it is a serious problem. Sibling sexual abuse is estimated to occur about five times more frequently than parent-child incest. Sibling incest is often more violent and angry than parent-child incest. Since it's widely underreported, the actual figures are probably much higher.

Sibling sexual abuse is not readily apparent. Out of fear and shame, a child will rarely volunteer information about it to parents or an outsider. If a child does say something about the abuse, chances are the incident will be dismissed as innocent exploration or as an act of mutual consent between peers. However, when it comes to sexual abuse, even a small age difference of a year or two negates the peer relationship between siblings.

A friend of mine was sexually molested by her brother. Afraid that her parents wouldn't believe her, she tried to tell the next-door neighbor what was happening. The neighbor cut her off, embarrassed, stammered something about how all little children "play doctor," and changed the subject. Jessica was 10 years old, and her brother 15. "I never brought it up again," Jessica said.

Children do "play doctor" and otherwise explore or investigate sex together. The typical age for this exploration, however, is much younger, usually between the ages of three and five. If this exploration occurs between two consenting siblings of about the same age, and if it is done out of innocence and curiosity, there is often no lingering damage other than, perhaps, some embarrassment later on.

Many siblings experience sexual feelings for each other. As Stephen

Bank and Michael Kahn write in *The Sibling Bond*, "In the process of sexual unfolding . . . brothers and sisters often admire, make comparisons and engage in sexually tinged play with one another." Societal and cultural prohibitions about sexual activity within families ensure that these feelings will ordinarily not be acted out. Almost every known society has incest taboos, which existed long before the study of genetics led humans to the realization that inbreeding was unhealthy for the species. It is assumed that these prohibitions were put into effect to protect the family unit and to ensure that people would leave their family of origin to form ties with other families, thereby strengthening the bonds in the larger community.

When parents make children feel bad about normal sexual feelings, the children will be tormented by guilt whenever they feel a sexual twinge around their siblings. By telling children they are "dirty" or "disgusting," or referring in an embarrassed way to parts of the body as "privates," the parents make the exploration of sex seem bad but at the same time enticing and mysterious. A developmental stage that might have passed normally without becoming a problem then becomes a problem.

My client Bobby, for example, was very close to his younger sister, Wendy, when they were growing up. Only a year apart in age, they would wrestle together, play games, and tell each other secrets. Their mother, who was very uptight about sex, forbade them to watch any love scenes on TV and also told them, rather mysteriously, that "thinking about it is just as bad as doing it," whatever "it" was.

One day Bobby opened the door to his sister's bedroom while she was changing her T-shirt. Overnight, it seemed, she had developed breasts, and the sight filled him with excitement. He quickly backed out and ran to his room, ashamed. Bobby figured he must be pretty disgusting—not only had he briefly thought about "it," he had thought about "it" with his sister! Bobby began avoiding Wendy, afraid that he would feel that way again. Wendy didn't understand why he wasn't her best friend anymore. "Our relationship was never the same after that," Bobby told me.

When the structure of the family breaks down because of parental conflict, drinking, drugs, violence, or emotional instability, then incest taboos are more likely to break down as well. Sometimes siblings in troubled homes seek each other out for comfort, and comfort turns to sex. More frequently, however, an older sibling, seething with rage, perhaps having been sexually abused himself, turns on a younger sibling and sexually molests her. These two types of incestuous experiences are what Bank and Kahn refer to in their book as Nurturance-Oriented Incest and Power-Oriented Incest. They explain, "Incest is more likely to occur if there is parental neglect or abandonment, so that brothers and sisters begin to need each other for solace, nurturance and identity, or as a vehicle to express rage and hurt."

If you experienced an incestuous sibling relationship, whether nurturing or power-oriented, chances are you are still consumed by guilt, depression, and self-hatred. Your trust in others, including your sibling, has been severely damaged.

Even though the incest occurred years ago, you and your sibling are probably still uncomfortable around each other because of the secret you share. If your sibling victimized you, you may still be afraid of him or her, or blame yourself for the abuse. In this chapter I'll discuss both parent-child incest and sibling incest and the effect such traumas have on the sibling relationship. I want to stress that I am focusing on just one area of the incest dynamic, the effects of sexual abuse on the sibling relationship. Furthermore, most of the cases I discuss here have involved years of therapy. If you have been sexually abused or have been an abuser, I strongly urge you to seek therapy. This subject deserves a whole book in itself, but until someone writes it, I hope the examples I discuss below will help you to begin healing your wounds.

"We Couldn't Talk About What Was Going On": How Parental Sexual Abuse Damages the Sibling Relationship

When parents sexually abuse their children, they use a variety of ruses to keep them quiet, from threatening physical harm to making the child believe the incest is her fault. They may insist that the incest is normal or a sign of specialness or love. Children learn early not to talk about these events with anyone, not even a brother or sister, not even when the abused child knows the same thing is happening to her siblings.

As an adult, your sibling relationships are probably filled with shame, secrecy, self-blame, and anger. Since you didn't talk about the sexual abuse at the time it was happening, you may feel an enormous distance between you and everyone else, including your siblings. This is what happened to my client Alicia and her two sisters.

Each of the sisters was sexually abused by their father from the time they were 6 or 7 until each was about 12. None talked about what was happening, nor did their mother seem to be aware of the abuse. She left the house early in the morning to do her errands, or was in the kitchen fixing dinner when her husband took one of his daughters into the bathroom for her daily "bath."

As adults, all three sisters were sexually promiscuous and had drinking or drug problems. Alicia's younger sister, Denise, had a young daughter whose father was unknown, and Denise was currently living with yet another boyfriend. Her older sister, Christine, in her late thirties, and Denise, in her late twenties, both still lived in Alicia's hometown in Wisconsin, while Alicia had moved to California. The three sisters rarely talked on the phone, and when they did, they spoke only about work, the weather, or old friends.

Alicia's distance from her sisters didn't seem odd to her, since, as she said, she "didn't have much to say" to anyone. Alicia was a loner. She picked up men in bars when she was drunk or doing drugs, had sex with them, and never saw them again. She didn't trust women; she avoided the other cocktail waitresses in the restaurant where she worked.

After her second suicide attempt, Alicia sought therapy. Each week she would come in for her session in costume. One week she would be dressed like a hooker, the next like a little girl. Her costume determined how she behaved in the session. She frequently smelled of alcohol, even though our appointments were early in the day. When I asked her questions about her background, she told me about her childhood in a sing-song voice. She recounted even the most hurtful things, such as her mother's complete disinterest in her, in a voice devoid of real feelings. It took a year for Alicia to learn to trust me, and then the costumes stopped. The sing-song voice came and went. One day I asked her why she was so promiscuous, and she broke down and told me about her father.

When we first started talking about the sexual abuse, she went on a few drinking and drug binges. After a few months, however, she could see that the drinking wasn't making the pain go away any longer, and she began attending A.A. meetings. Within a few months she stopped drinking and taking drugs altogether.

Over a period of a few years, while she worked through the pain of the abuse, she was flooded by memories that she had blocked. Many of those memories revolved around her two sisters, and how each had looked away when one came out from her "bath," how no one spoke when their father came into the room and called for one of his girls.

"I guess we were always hoping the other one would be called," Alicia said. "I know I was. But when he chose one of them, then I would feel guilty. At some point I just forgot all about it."

Alicia was angry that she and her sisters had been deprived of any chance for closeness or friendship. She wrote them each a letter describing her feelings and what she had been discovering in therapy. Along with each letter she sent a book on sexual abuse. She added that she would love to talk to them and would be coming to Madison in a month.

Christine called Alicia as soon as she got the letter. She was so drunk, Alicia could barely understand what she was saying, but the gist of it was that Christine couldn't wait to talk about that "filthy bastard father of ours."

Denise didn't respond to Alicia's letter. When Alicia called after a couple of weeks and asked if she'd received the letter, Denise said she didn't remember abuse happening in their childhood and quickly got off the phone.

One of the most powerful defenses that children have against sexual abuse is denial. But denial is also what gets most victims in trouble later in life and puts their own children at risk of abuse. Denise was in denial about her sexual abuse, and she was allowing her six-year-old daughter, Candy, to spend the night at her parents' home while she and her boyfriend hit the bars. When Alicia came to Madison, one of the first things she did was talk to Denise's little girl. Yes, she told Aunt Alicia, she was getting a "bath" from Grandpa every night.

Alicia let her sisters know what was going on with Denise's little girl. Everything flooded out after that, even for Denise, who finally broke down and kept saying over and over, "I remember, I remember."

Two days after Alicia arrived, she and Christine confronted their father about the sexual abuse. Denise was too afraid to accompany them. Their father emphatically denied everything; their mother was aghast. She accused them of being wicked children with dirty minds. Their parents' reactions only strengthened the bond between Alicia and Christine.

When Alicia came back to California, she felt hopeful. For her two sisters, the healing was beginning, and she had made a connection with both of them.

Christine found a group for survivors of sexual abuse in Madison, but her drinking escalated as she started to deal with her own pain. She and Alicia talked every few days, and Christine said her memories were threatening to overwhelm her. Alicia encouraged her to stick with it, that it would get better with time.

Three months after her return to California, Alicia discovered that Denise had been leaving Candy with their parents again and was drinking so much that she was unable to care for her daughter. She called Denise and gave her two options: send Candy to California to stay with

Alicia, or Alicia would call the police and have the girl taken away. Two days later, Candy was in Los Angeles.

Alicia continues to work on healing her own wounds. Having Candy living with her has been a financial and emotional drain but has helped her healing. "I've been able to mother Candy in a way that I wish I had been mothered. Nurturing feels good on both sides," she said to me. Christine has visited California twice and is thinking about moving there, but she's told Alicia that she won't come until she's achieved at least one year of sobriety. Denise keeps in touch with Candy but hasn't come out to visit. She calls Alicia sometimes when she's drunk and feeling vulnerable. In those conversations, Denise talks about what happened when they were kids and says she wishes she could be stronger like her two sisters. Alicia listens, but never pushes. She still hopes for her sister's recovery.

What You Can Do

When you begin to heal the wounds of your own abuse, reach out to your brother or sister. Confronting the truth together and sharing your pain will break down the barriers between you. The scars from sexual abuse are deep and enduring, and feeling mistrustful of others is one of the many prices you pay. Opening yourself up to your sibling can be the beginning of the rebuilding of that trust.

You cannot force your sibling to break down her own denial; each person has to cope with the fact of sexual abuse herself, on her own time schedule. Trying to force your sibling to acknowledge incest when she isn't yet strong enough can be damaging.

You and your sibling may decide you want to confront, together, the person who abused you. You will definitely feel stronger if you do this together and can offer each other support. You can compose a letter together, or have a face-to-face confrontation with the abuser.

Be sure also to discuss the parent who "didn't see" what was going on in your home. Confronting the truth of the abuse is painful, but you also have to face the real possibility that your other parent knew what was going on and denied or ignored it. Having the support of your sibling during this painful time is another important part of your healing process.

Parent each other. Maybe you are afraid of physical contact, such as hugging, because it has been used against you in the past. Now, try to hug your sibling, or allow your sibling to hug you. Sit close together while you talk. Learning to trust physical touch is healthy and healing; learning to trust a warm human touch will be a positive step for both of you.

"I Thought There Was Something Wrong with Me": When Siblings Deny Parental Sexual Abuse

Sometimes a parent (or other adult) molests only one child and leaves the other children in the family alone. If you were sexually abused and your sibling was not, you have grown up in the same house but in a different world.

Gretchen initially came into therapy to work on her relationship with her boyfriend. Fearing that he was going to leave her, she would cling to him, inventing problems for which she demanded his help. The more demands she made on him, the more he distanced himself from her; in turn the more clingy and desperate she became. He always ended up running away from her, and Gretchen would feel guilty for pushing him away.

Her boyfriend, evasive and angry, refused to come in for joint counseling and refused to give her any reassurance. Instead he kept backing away from Gretchen and blaming her for the problems in their relationship. As we talked about her history, she revealed the sexual abuse she experienced as a child. Gretchen realized for the first time that what she was doing with her boyfriend mirrored her relationship with her older brother, Jim.

Gretchen's father had sexually molested her from the time she was 10 years old. Although her parents were divorced and her mother had custody of the children, her father showed up every weekend to take them to his home. Every night that she stayed at her father's house, he molested her. Most of the time she pretended she was sleeping. Once she protested, and he told her that if she said anything about it she would be sent away to a home for disturbed children, because no one would believe her. He also told her that she should realize how "special" she was because he, her father, paid so much attention to her.

Gretchen's father had an entirely different relationship with Jim. He took his son on hunting and fishing trips, came to all his baseball games, and otherwise acted like a proud, interested parent.

Jim had avoided Gretchen for most of her life—probably, Gretchen had thought, because she was a "loser." But as Gretchen focused on their relationship in therapy, she realized that Jim must have known or suspected what was going on and pushed her away. That way he would never have to see his father in a different light.

Gretchen recalled that when the abuse first started, she went into Jim's room, upset and hoping to talk with him. He got angry and pushed her literally out of the room. Once she broke down and cried in his room, but he ran out and left her sobbing alone on the edge of his bed.

Gretchen became agitated and angry as she talked about these incidents. Now, instead of feeling dirty, she felt betrayed. One night she called Jim and said she wanted to speak with him about what had happened, but he angrily denied knowing what she was talking about. He even told her not to call him again. Jim was unable or unwilling to admit that he knew about the abuse. His response to his sister's pain was complete denial. Understanding this, Gretchen was now no longer willing to continue the relationship she had with either her father or her brother as long as they refused to acknowledge what happened to her. When she saw that her boyfriend would probably never commit to her and was using her behavior as an excuse to remain distant, she broke up with him, too.

Gretchen's life was lonely and scary for some time. Cut off from her family and without her boyfriend, she struggled with depression and weight gain. Over a period of several years, however, Gretchen created healthy relationships with a new group of friends. She lost the weight she had put on during the difficult times and tentatively entered a relationship with a man she believed trustworthy.

Changing Your Relationship

If Gretchen's story resembles the pattern of abuse in your family, there may be nothing you can do to make your sibling acknowledge what took place. If your sibling won't listen to you and admit his or her own feelings of helplessness and fear in turning away from you when you most needed help, there is no possibility for an honest, trusting relationship with your sibling. Your best position is to remove yourself from this sibling emotionally—and physically if necessary—until a time when he or she decides to accept the truth of your memories and your feelings about them. I must warn you, however, that this may never happen.

Your sibling may also put his own relationship needs first and choose not to change his relationship with and feelings about your parent(s)—even though he acknowledges the truth about the abuse. In this case, also, you will probably have to let go of the sibling relationship and continue to work on having more healthy relationships with others in your future.

Just because you have been denied a healthy family, you should not be condemned to never having a family; work toward making your friends into family.

What You Can Do If Your Sibling Talks with You About the Abuse

Sometimes, after an initial phase of denial, siblings will acknowledge that sexual abuse did occur. If you find yourself in the position of hearing your sibling tell you about being sexually abused, listen to her and believe her. Most of all, don't expect her to heal overnight. Many siblings are supportive when they first hear of the abuse, yet find it difficult to continue offering support over time. You may be tempted to say things like, "When are you going to get on with your life?" "When will you let the family get back to normal?" "Isn't it about time you got over it?" But before you say those things, consider how long your sister has carried her secret and how painful her childhood has been. You can tell her that it's difficult and painful to listen to the details of the abuse. If you feel anger at the abuser, say so. If you feel overwhelmed, tell your sister that the subject is too painful for you right now but that you want her to talk about it again soon. Set up specific times when she can tell you what she needs to say. Ask her what she wants from you. A hug? A listener? An angry avenger? Someone to tell her it's going to be okay now?

Of course, your abused sibling's revelations will mean you will have to examine the abuser in a different light. This won't be easy if you once enjoyed a happy and uncomplicated relationship with him or her. Be sure to tell your sibling how hard the situation is for you, too. It may be difficult for *her* to hear *you* when she is overwhelmed by her own pain, but as she heals she will find it easier to understand and empathize with your feelings, too.

"At Least He Paid Attention to Me": When Older Siblings Take Advantage of Younger Siblings

A familiar pattern of sibling incest is for older siblings to make younger ones "partners" in sex and swear them to secrecy, often by threatening them with violence. Although older sisters also abuse younger siblings, the most common perpetrator of sibling sexual abuse is a brother, older by three to ten years. Rarely does a sibling fight back from sibling abuse; most of the time the victim pretends to be sleeping or just gives in.

Beverly Engel, an expert on sexual abuse and the author of *The Right to Innocence,* told me that she has seen clients, abused by an older sibling, who "even as early as age two knew it was wrong. Since many older siblings who abuse their younger siblings have been sexually abused themselves, they bring to the abuse of the younger sibling a Pandora's box of shame and guilt, which the younger sibling picks up." She added that the younger the child is, the more damaging incest experiences are.

Younger children desperately want their older siblings to like and approve of them. If parents are neglectful or abusive, the older sibling's acceptance becomes far more important than normal. But if older children have learned abusive behavior from their parents, or haven't received the love they need, they won't know how to give love to their younger siblings. If older children have been treated like objects, they will treat younger children in the family as objects as well. It is common for older siblings who have been sexually molested to turn their anger onto younger siblings and molest them.

Barry was in his forties when he entered therapy. He was married with two sons, aged 11 and 6. He was anxious, needy, and desperate to please. His insecurities got in the way of his functioning in an assertive way at work or with his wife. His wife was a disapproving, critical, and self-absorbed woman. She nagged Barry to be more assertive at work—to "stop being such a wimp"—because he wasn't making enough money. Barry spent a lot of time worrying about her and her needs to the exclusion of his own.

Barry had been in therapy about six months when he started talking about his young son, Shawn. As Shawn approached age seven, Barry became more and more agitated, angry, and anxious. He worried about where the child was and what he was doing, who he was with. One day he told me he was suspicious of his older son, Max. I asked him what he meant, suspicious about what? Barry then told me that no older boy could be trusted, that no innocent seven-year-old could survive in the world without becoming a victim of "some pervert."

Where were these thoughts coming from? At first I suspected Barry was warding off his own sexual feelings toward Shawn, but then I asked him if he had had any sexual experiences when he was seven.

"I vowed never to talk about it," he said, "but I had some sexual experiences with my older brother about then."

I asked if perhaps those experiences had something to do with how Barry was feeling about his sons.

"Maybe," he said. Then he reassured me that he and his brother got along "swell" and that the sex was just something silly that had happened years ago.

As we talked more, however, a picture of Barry emerged as a small, clumsy kid who worshipped his brother, Ron, a handsome guy five years his senior. Ron initiated sex with Barry when Barry was seven, and Barry went along with it. "That was the only time I got attention from anybody," Barry said. "No one ever hugged or even touched each other in my family. My father was rarely there at all."

We discussed the differences in age, and I suggested that his brother had taken unfair advantage of Barry's needs for attention and affection; that his brother had used him. Barry insisted that he was as much at fault as his brother. "I didn't mind it—the sex part. Sometimes I liked it. I can't blame him. I never said no."

"But your brother betrayed your trust," I said. "It doesn't matter if you liked it or not." Barry didn't believe me, so I tried a different approach. I asked him how he would feel if Max did the same thing to Shawn. Then Barry got angry. By imagining incest happening to someone else he loved, he could see how manipulative and uncaring his brother had been.

Barry had initially described his relationship with Ron as close, but now he realized that their shared sexual experience was "a metaphor for our relationship in total." Barry was always giving and Ron was taking. Ron never volunteered anything. "He calls me if he needs something or wants to brag about himself, but when I call him, he's not interested in how I'm doing," Barry said.

For Barry to recognize his brother's narcissism was a good first step. He decided to talk to his brother about the incest. When he finally found the courage to do so, Ron was not even defensive. His attitude was, "So what?" In the face of such disinterest, Barry was discouraged and changed the subject. His last illusions of closeness to Ron crumbled.

He decided not to call his brother anymore. "Let him call me," he said. It took six months for Ron to pick up the phone.

During that six months, Barry stopped feeling guilty and responsible. Instead he felt angry and hurt. His brother had taken advantage of him to gratify his own needs. His whole understanding of his brother had shifted, and now Barry was heartbroken. "He was the only one in my family whom I thought cared, and now it turns out that was a lie, too," he said.

When Ron finally called, he acted as if they had spoken yesterday and that nothing was wrong or different between them. In the course of the conversation he made vague, uncomfortable references to "the crazy things kids do."

Barry told him that he now saw their relationship in a different light. Ron yelled into the telephone, "Mother showed me off like I was some product; she was always saying, 'Look at me! Look at what I produced!' And *you* thought I was perfect, too. You could never imagine that I might have a problem, too."

The rest of the phone call was spent discussing the time their aunt had fondled Ron when he was a youngster. They never got back to what had happened between Barry and Ron. In retrospect Barry realized that Ron had again shifted the attention to himself and avoided talking about what had happened with Barry. In subsequent phone calls, whenever Barry brought up the sibling incest, Ron shifted into talking about his experience with their aunt.

"I'm angry," Barry said, "but I don't want the relationship to end over what happened. I'm willing to hang in with Ron. I want him to understand how I feel. I still can't believe that he won't someday understand my feelings. That's too painful for me to comprehend at this point."

A few months later, Barry insisted that Ron *listen* to him, not about the sexual abuse, but in general. Ron attempted to do so, but Barry still has to police every conversation, because Ron's tendency is to shift the subject back to himself.

Before, Barry was unable to recognize self-absorbed people. He never noticed when people monopolized conversations and failed to ask anything about him. He married a self-absorbed woman and surrounded himself with friends who were just like his brother. Unfortunately, when Barry made demands on his wife to equalize their relationship, she was unwilling to change. They eventually separated. Barry feels confident that his next relationship will be a more caring, equitable one.

What You Can Do

If you have blamed yourself for the abuse inflicted by an older sibling, your first step is to understand that you are blameless. You cannot be held accountable for what occurred between you and an older sibling. Whether the sex was sometimes pleasurable is irrelevant. You were abused, used, and taken advantage of. When you first acknowledge that your sibling has used you, you will feel hurt, then angry. If you want to continue your relationship, you will have to confront these feelings and, most likely, tell your brother or sister about them.

If your sibling continues to deny responsibility, you cannot force him to acknowledge your reality, but you do have a choice as to whether you want to continue a relationship with someone who has hurt and victimized you.

Look at your current relationships and determine if, like Barry's, they have abusive aspects to them. If you have been in denial about the sexual abuse, you may be repeating elements of the abuse in your current relationships.

Moreover, the abuse or neglect in your home that led your sibling to abuse you has also had its own separate negative effects on you. Again, evaluate your current relationships to assess whether you use sex as a way of getting affection. Many children who have been sexually abused use sex as the only way they know to share physical closeness. Learn to ask directly for affection, rather than for sex.

"I'm Disgusted with Myself": When Siblings Face the Truth About Their Own Abusive Behavior

Unlike Ron, some siblings feel guilty and ashamed for having hurt or taken advantage of their younger siblings. Often when these people enter a 12-step recovery program or get into therapy, these feelings reemerge.

I saw Jack in therapy soon after he entered Alcoholics Anonymous. He had been alcoholic since the age of 12. His parents were both alcoholic and abusive. He had been sexually molested by a friend of the family when he was 10. Jack had dulled the turmoil of his feelings with alcohol and now, in his mid-thirties, was finally experiencing the pain of his own childhood. As he started progressing in the A.A. program, his sponsor had him make a list of all the people whom he had "wronged" so that he could make amends. The first person on Jack's list was his sister, Sherry, who was three years younger than Jack.

Sherry was a cocaine addict and alcoholic. She, too, had been drinking and using drugs since the age of 12 or 13. Jack and his sister had occasionally hung out together when their parents were drunk and abusive, but mostly they had withdrawn into themselves, not knowing how to talk about what they were feeling. They had their separate friends, and both spent lots of time away from home. It never occurred to Jack to take care of Sherry, because no one had ever taken care of him. He didn't know what love and nurturing he was missing, so he couldn't give it to anyone else.

Jack now confessed to me that when his sister was 12 and he was 15, he had come home from a party drunk and had forced her to have sex with him. She had put up a little resistance, and then just gave in and waited it out. She never told on him, they never talked about it, and it never happened again, but from that moment on, they avoided each other.

I encouraged Jack to talk to Sherry about the incident. After thinking it over a few months, he called and asked to get together with her. When he showed up at her apartment, Sherry was drunk. He told me later that it was the first time in almost 20 years that he had been in his sister's presence sober.

He told her about the 12-step program and then brought up their teenage sexual incident. Sherry shook her head and said she didn't want to talk about it, but he insisted. He told her how sorry he was and how guilty and ashamed he felt for what had happened.

She wasn't able to say much that night, but later she told Jack that she had felt "dirty" when the incest occurred and had been sure it was her fault. When Jack withdrew from her afterward, she thought it was because he found her disgusting. She was uncomfortable talking about what had happened—not because she thought Jack should feel bad, but because of her own self-hatred.

Jack encouraged Sherry to get into Cocaine Anonymous or Alcoholics Anonymous. He offered to take her to a meeting, but she declined. He worried that he was responsible for her drinking and drugs. "I let you down," he told her. "I could have been a good older brother, one person in your life who treated you right, and I screwed up royally."

"Don't flatter yourself, Jack," she said. "We weren't close before that thing happened and we weren't close after. Let's face it, we just didn't impact much on each other, one way or the other."

Sherry, as Jack could see, was numb to her feelings. What Jack had to understand was that he could not make amends by trying to rescue her. In aggressively attempting to reform Sherry, he would be making an effort to make himself feel better, but it wouldn't help Sherry. Jack had to let go of that feeling of responsibility. He told Sherry that he wanted to try being friends, and that he wouldn't pressure her to stop drinking.

She laughed, and said, "I guess you forgot, it's a drag hanging out with straight people. They don't know how to have fun." He laughed, too, and left. In my office later that week, he cried. How sad it was, he told me, that he and his sister had been so damaged. But he was hopeful. "I never thought *I* would change."

For Sherry, her whole growing-up experience had been one of betrayal, neglect, and abuse; the forced sex was one more indignity piled on all the others she suffered. Sherry never accepted Jack's admission of his own brutality.

Jack could not make Sherry's problems disappear. He could only accept responsibility for what he had done. Today he continues to work on self-forgiveness. "Sherry can't forgive me, because she doesn't even realize what a terrible thing I did," he said. Although in therapy I did not let Jack off the hook for his behavior, I helped him to understand the incident within the context of the family's home life. Jack now realizes he is not completely responsible for his sister's problems.

Jack keeps in touch with Sherry and lets her define the boundaries of their relationship. He's working on staying sober and, as he puts it, "trying to be a good person."

Changing Your Relationship

Your first step is to admit to your sibling what you did and to apologize for it. Encourage her to tell you how she feels, and listen to whatever emotions well up in her: anger, hurt, shame, guilt. Let her talk as much as she needs to; don't push your guilt on her or try to get her to feel sorry for you. Most important, don't force her forgiveness.

Back off, if that's what she wants. You cannot force her to hear you out, nor to forgive you. If your sibling's anger and betrayal are such that she cannot forgive you, you must accept this; remember, at the same time, that people are capable of change.

Living with the knowledge of what you have done is your burden, not your sibling's. Accepting the responsibility for the abuse means you're on the road to eventually forgiving yourself.

"We Loved Each Other More Than Anyone Else": When Sibling Love Crosses Over into Incest

Sometimes siblings in troubled, abusive homes form a strong bond of attachment and loyalty. Such siblings may cling to each other, closing out the rest of the world. In time, their unfulfilled needs for affection, love, and touch may create an incestuous relationship. This kind of incest is generally mutual, coming as it does from a feeling of love, connection, and need.

Nevertheless, siblings who cross over into incest, even nurturant incest, suffer consequences. Aware that what they are doing is considered bad and wrong, they hide their feelings from the world. Although they may express defiance, usually they also feel guilty, ashamed, and perverse.

Mary came into therapy because she was unable to get along with her brother's wife, and this was causing friction in her relationship with her brother—the only relationship, she quickly told me, that mattered to her.

During the initial phases of therapy, Mary primarily wanted me to help her get rid of Frank's wife. How, Mary wanted to know, could she convince Frank that his wife was a horrible person? Eventually Mary expressed rage at Frank for getting married in the first place. She wanted to hurt him, she told me, like he had hurt her.

Mary had no close friends other than Frank. Her pattern was to seduce married men at work, especially men who normally wouldn't get involved in an affair. After having sex with them, she was consumed with guilt, self-hatred, and disgust for doing something that was "morally wrong." She told me, however, that she felt powerless to stop these relationships.

She lived in the same apartment building as her brother, and they saw each other every day before and after work. She always told Frank the details of her affairs. I questioned her about her brother's involvement in her sexual life. After about a year of seeing me, she revealed the depth of her relationship with Frank and why she felt so betrayed by him.

Mary was 11 months older than Frank, and they had clung together as kids. They slept together when their parents didn't come home at night. They defended each other from their mother's verbal and their father's physical abuse. By the time they were teenagers, they were having intercourse regularly. They made no other friends and were together constantly, except when they attended separate classes at school. From the beginning, Mary said, she had felt guilty because she was the older one. But she didn't want to let go of the sexual part of their relationship.

They continued their sexual relationship until Frank joined the Army after high school. This was the first blow Mary experienced. Then, while Frank was in Germany, he met his future wife, married her, and moved back to his hometown.

Once Frank returned, he and Mary never discussed their past sexual relationship. Frank didn't seem troubled by what had happened, but Mary had been shocked that he had moved on to another woman and left her behind so easily.

Mary was bonded to her brother as she was to no one else in her life. She felt tremendous guilt and shame, yet she compared every man she met to Frank. Of course, none ever measured up. She had lived in a fantasy, believing that her relationship with Frank would always be intimate. She felt "dirty," but she still had continuing sexual fantasies about her brother. She could not progress with her life or accept Frank's marriage.

Mary acted seductive with Frank in front of his wife, but she always ended up feeling rejected. On his part, Frank didn't seem to know quite what to do. When Mary had male visitors, Frank was embarrassed by her flagrant sexual conduct, especially after she had been drinking. They never talked about any of these feelings.

I suggested to Mary that she talk to her brother and try to get their feelings out in the open. I reminded her that she and Frank talked about everything else and had a close, supportive, loving relationship. Mary was terrified of bringing up the subject, however. When I asked why, she said, "He's going to get angry that I talked about it and leave me."

Finally one evening, Frank's wife, who usually was quiet and shy, told both Frank and Mary that she was shocked by Mary's behavior toward her brother and left the room. Mary, stunned, told Frank that they needed to talk. He got his coat and they left the apartment to take a walk around the block. Mary spilled out her feelings of confusion and abandonment.

Frank, holding her hand, explained that once he left home, the sexual part of the relationship was over. "We weren't kids anymore, and it would have been wrong to keep on doing that," he said.

"But you keep rejecting me," she said, crying.

"I don't know what to do when you come on like that," Frank said. "I'm afraid Inga is going to find out about what we did as kids, and she'll be disgusted with both of us."

"So, you think I'm disgusting," Mary said.

Frank stopped walking and said quietly, "Sometimes I feel that what we did was kind of sick. I wish I didn't, but I can't help it."

"I feel that way too," Mary said.

That was the beginning for Frank and Mary. They could both finally wash away their feelings of guilt and shame together. I helped Mary to see the incest within the context of their home life. She and Frank were then able to talk about their childhood again, without that unspoken "thing" between them. Mary had to work for several years to change her seductive behavior with men and her addiction to destructive relationships. The more she placed her relationship with Frank into perspective, the less need she felt to repeat those confused feelings of sexual guilt and shame.

What You Can Do

I suggest that you bring the relationship with your sibling out into the open. If your sexual relationship has continued into adulthood, you will have to stop it if you want to "mainstream" your relationship. By continuing a sexual relationship with your sibling, you are closing others out of your life, and probably depriving yourself of the chance of a healthy, intimate relationship.

Talk about why your relationship turned sexual. What was missing in your home that drew the two of you together? What were you looking for in a sexual relationship? Chances are you will talk about things like closeness, warmth, acceptance, nurturing—all things that were probably missing in your home. Realize that these qualities are necessary to your emotional and even physical survival. Understand that these were the empty spaces you were trying to fill through sex.

Expand your circle of relationships and look for nurturing and love in other people besides your sibling. Don't compare every relationship with the one you had with your sibling. Let each relationship in the present stand on its own merits.

Distinguish clearly between affection and sex. When you want affection, don't be seductive. When you want affection and your partner wants sex, say so. Say you want to be cuddled and held. Your feelings about nurturing, affection, and sex have been confused, and you will need to work on separating them.

To aid you in your recovery, seek out self-help groups for the survivors of sexual abuse. Talking with others who have experienced sexual abuse, or who have abused a sibling or others, can be part of your healing.

In working through your relationship with your sibling, you will begin healing the wounds from sexual abuse. If you have been abused by a sibling and have decided to stop contact with him, this decision will empower you and help you in your determination not to continue being a victim, but rather, to be a *survivor* of sexual abuse.

It will take you a long time to develop the trust that has been broken or was never allowed to develop in your family. Be patient and loving to yourself during these difficult years. Don't push yourself to progess any faster than you can.

CHAPTER TEN

Moving into the Future

Helping Your Children Form Healthy Sibling Relationships

By working out your sibling relationship, you have chosen to unravel one of the most powerful relationships of your life. In doing so, you've had the opportunity to learn more about yourself, your siblings, and your family of origin, and you have been able to heal and integrate your past. Carrying your relationship with your siblings into adulthood, you have finally left your childhood behind and moved fully into the present.

Resolving your sibling relationship can take any of a number of forms. Perhaps, for you, resolution has meant saying goodbye to an abusive sibling who will not change. Or perhaps it has meant confronting a manipulative sibling and demanding change, negotiating a truce with a fiercely competitive sibling, or otherwise working together with a sympathetic and understanding sibling to untangle your relationship and bring it into the present.

Whatever course your relationship has taken, one thing is sure: taking steps to resolve a troubled sibling relationship may not always bring you closer to your brother or sister, but the process will bring you closer to yourself. By evaluating what you and your sibling can or cannot change, and what each of you is willing or unwilling to accept in your current relationship, you will inevitably define your own goals and expectations, not only for your relationship with your brother or sister but for your other relationships as well.

I have seen similar developments time and again: A client resolves his rivalrous relationship with his brother and suddenly his boss, whom he used to see as oppressive and demanding, no longer drives him crazy. Another client bridges an angry relationship with her sister and is able to make friends with women again. Still another client, who has confronted her brother about abusing his favored status, soon finds herself demanding more respect in other areas of her life as well.

But there is another benefit to resolving your sibling relationship. Once you understand what makes siblings tick, you'll be in a much better position to help your own children forge satisfying relationships. What could be more rewarding than to be able to take all you have learned and pass it on to the next generation?

The Next Generation: Helping Your Kids Get Along

Sisters and Brothers is a how-to book for resolving sibling relationships. But it can also be read as a how-not-to book for parents who want to raise children to have rewarding sibling relationships. Understanding how favoritism, competition, labeling, and abuse can make it difficult or impossible for siblings to get along will help you to avoid these problems with your children.

Since children learn by example, working at a healthy, open, loving relationship with your sibling is one of the best ways to help your sons and daughters with their own sibling relationships. If that's not possible because your sibling is abusive, remember that it's also valuable to show your kids how to stand up for themselves.

In the following sections I'll provide questions to help you diagnose which of your own sibling problems you may be encouraging your children to repeat, as well as strategies for breaking these cycles.

Removing the Obstacle of Parental Expectations

Parents put obstacles in their children's path by burdening them with expectations. As we saw in Chapter Two, your parents' expectations, spoken or not, seriously affected your sibling relationships.

Following are some questions you and your partner can ask yourselves in order to learn whether you may be putting similar obstacles in the way of your children. You may expect them to act a certain way with you or with each other, or you may expect too much of them in general.

Do you expect your kids to get along no matter what?

Do you expect your older children to always be "good" big brothers or sisters?

Do you expect your younger children to always respect or listen to their older siblings?

Do you expect your children to meet your needs for friendship, reassurance, or attention—needs that would be better met by another adult?

Do you expect your children to mend your marriage?

Discovering your own expectations is the first step to removing the barriers you may be placing in your children's path. If you and your siblings were busy satisfying your parents' expectations, you may not have learned to recognize or ask for what you need. Similarly, your expectations of your children may be somewhat hidden.

If you find yourself expecting to be nourished by your children—other than by the sheer joy of having them—it's time to look inside yourself to see how you might get your needs met elsewhere. You may have to take a hard look at your marriage as well, to discover what is needed in that relationship.

Talk about your feelings with your partner. Frank communication is essential to a healthy spousal relationship. It is equally important to establish friendships or join a parents' support group. Like everyone else, parents need support and a time to talk about themselves.

Teaching Healthy Resolution of Conflict

If you and your sibling were drawn into your parents' conflicts, those conflicts undoubtedly played havoc with your sibling relationship. Because you were raised with no healthy boundaries within your family, you've had to learn about the healthy separations between parents and children on your own. This is not an easy task, and you may find yourself unwittingly following in your parents' footsteps. Following are some questions you can ask yourself to determine if your children are becoming embroiled in your conflicts with your partner:

Do your children react with anxiety or with a need to please or distract you when you and your partner have a disagreement or become tense with each other?

Do you encourage your kids to take sides during your disagreements with your partner?

Do you talk to your children about your problems with your partner?

Do you make negative, angry, or demeaning remarks about your partner to your children?

Do you want your children to comfort you after you've had a disagreement with your partner?

Learning to fight in a productive way is a difficult assignment if you have never witnessed healthy conflict, but it can be done. Pay attention to your feelings about your children during times of stress with your partner. If you feel tempted to draw them into your conflicts, this is a sure sign that you are having a hard time expressing your own needs and feelings. Try to address your feelings of helplessness or frustration directly.

Consider reading books that can help you learn healthy ways to communicate your needs and feelings. You might also seek joint counseling with your partner. A therapist can teach you to resolve conflicts in a productive fashion and assist you in discovering your own stumbling blocks.

You and your partner may be tempted to overcompensate by never allowing your children to see that you have disagreements. You may be afraid that you will upset your children if you raise your voice or are a bit irritable with your mate. In this case you run the risk of promoting the myth of the always-happy family.

Learn to get comfortable with conflict. No relationship can exist without conflict. Show your children that it's normal to agree to disagree, it's normal to get angry, and anger can be talked through. Letting your children see that you and your partner can handle conflict, without involving the children, is essential. That's where the parenting books come in handy.

Encouraging Healthy Competition

Competition flows down through the generations and is a difficult pattern to break. Whether you were raised in a highly competitive atmosphere or one where no competition was allowed, you face the task of finding a healthy middle ground for your children. Here are some questions to help you evaluate how you and your partner are handling this sensitive parenting issue.

Do you expect your children to perform for you?

Do you withhold love or approval based on performance?

Do you give more attention to the child who competes successfully?

Do your kids clamor, push, and shove each other to get your attention?

Are you disappointed, on your behalf, when your child doesn't win?

Do you say things to your children like, "Your sister was faster when she was your age," or "Whoever gets an A in math gets ten dollars," or "Are you going to let your brother beat you?"

Do you brag to others about how well your child performs?

Do you compete with other parents over how well your children are doing?

Everyone will probably answer yes to some of these questions, at least some of the time, as it's hard to separate our egos completely from our children. Sometimes it's hard to distinguish between being proud of our kids and taking ownership of what they've done. This is a lifelong job each parent has to struggle with. But if you or your partner answered yes to more than two or three of these questions, it's time to step back and change some of your behavior.

Your goal is to keep your ego and your children's achievements separate. Instead of always praising their successes and criticizing their failures, ask your children how *they* feel about their performance in any given situation. Did they try their best? If you find yourself desperately wanting your kid to win at something, curb your desire to communicate that hope. Let your kids know that whatever they achieve is up to them; you have no fixed agenda. In so doing, you help them to become inner-directed. Also, encourage your children to be supportive of one another's efforts.

If you came from a highly competitive home, you may find yourself overcompensating with your own children. If your first impulse is to discourage any competition, it's time for you to learn what healthy competition looks like. Try going to some Little League or youth soccer games. Notice those kids who don't shy away from competition but aren't fanatical about winning either. Observe how these children and their parents interact. In doing so, you will get a clearer picture of how to foster robust, fun competition with your kids.

Putting Favoritism to Rest

If you were raised in a home where your parents favored one child over another, you know how favoritism can poison the sibling relationship. Yet favoritism runs in families, so you might find yourself falling into the same trap. The following questions will help you to find out if you're slipping into some familiar patterns with your kids:

Do you take one child's side in conflicts between your children?

Do you spend more time with one child?

Do you buy one child more clothes or give her more money?

Do you dislike one of your children?

Do you feel more empathy for, and therefore give more attention to, one child in particular?

Do you turn to a particular child to get affection you feel you aren't getting from your partner?

If you answered yes to even one of these questions, take a step back to figure out where in your own history your response is coming from.

You may feel that your favoritism is justified or that you can't fight what seems to be a gut reaction to your children. But don't give in to those feelings. If you do, there is a good chance your behaviors will have a harmful effect on your children individually and will damage their sibling relationship as well.

Find ways to acknowledge all of your children for their own specialness. Don't give in to the temptation to single out one for special attention or for abuse. If your partner favors one child or makes a child into a black sheep, talk about what's going on. Offer support and understanding, but insist that your partner get help.

Explore why you feel a particular way about a particular child. Is the child you favor a "runt" like you were? Do you like the child who is the prettiest because she makes you feel pretty? Exploring your own feelings about the child you favor and the child you disfavor may help you uncover the roots of your own pain about being the favored or disfavored child in your family of origin.

If you've been raised with favoritism, you may overcompensate by taking excessive care to treat your children exactly alike. In so doing you may make too big a deal of equality. Recognize the specialness in each of your children, and don't be afraid to praise one child at any particular moment.

Peeling Away Labels

Labeling is a technique we all use to define our world. But be careful when you catch yourself thinking of your children in set ways. You are on your way to limiting how you view them, which in turn will restrict their personalities. Monitor yourself by asking these questions periodically:

Do you compare your children to one another?

Do you describe your children by using the same labels over and over?

Have you come to expect certain behaviors from your children?

Do you discourage your children from attempting something new—a sport, a class, a different haircut—because it doesn't match your picture of who they are?

Do you allot your children separate domains?

If you answered yes to any of these questions, go out of your way to find traits in your children that you never noticed before, and make a special effort not to use the labels you turn to automatically.

If you were raised in an angry, negative household, pay particular attention to the way you feel about your kids when you're angry. You have been trained to lash out. To avoid the name-calling, labeling, and comparing you grew up with, you need to identify and express your feelings toward your children in a more productive way.

Do your best to see your children, not as who you want them to be, but as who they are, just as you would have wished your parents and siblings could have seen you. Your own children, if you let them, may surprise you. And those very surprises are a wonderful gift.

Curbing Abusive Behavior

Abuse steals dignity, self-esteem, and a sense of control from the lives of children. Any form of abusive behavior is damaging to children and their sibling relationship. If you were abused, you owe it to your children not to repeat the abuse that was heaped on you. Following are some questions to ask yourself to see how well you are channeling the angry feelings that are the legacy of your childhood:

Do you spank your children when you are frustrated with them?

Do you yell or shake them if they don't respond to you in the way you wish?

Do you lash out at your child when you feel tired or frustrated?

Do you sometimes feel out of control and hit or scream at your child?

Do you sometimes just want to hurt your child because your anger is so big?

Have you punished your child by locking him or her into a room for long periods of time?

Have you bruised your children, hit them with an object, pushed, shoved, or kicked them?

Have you left a young child alone for more than three minutes?

Have you, out of anger or depression, neglected to feed, change, bathe, or otherwise nurture your child?

If you answered yes to any of these questions, get professional help or find a support group as soon as possible. You cannot work on this problem alone. You need support while you work through your feelings of helplessness and anger. In the support group you will learn ways to control your anger—for instance, by walking away, counting to 10, deep breathing, hitting a pillow, recognizing your anger before it gets to the point of explosion. You will also be surrounded by people who understand your feelings because they have been through similar experiences.

One way that parents overcompensate for their own abusive childhoods is to become overly permissive with their children. They don't understand limits themselves, or they want to give their children freedoms they never had.

One of my clients, who had been beaten and silenced by her father whenever she talked above a whisper, found herself unable to put any restrictions on her children at all. After a long flight during which her kids ran roughshod over the whole plane, she returned home determined to learn how to set boundaries on her children's behavior. Like this client, you too can set limits for your children without abusing them. In fact, children thrive on a rational structure; chaos frightens them.

Having no boundaries or limits for your children is not a healthy alternative to the restrictive way in which you were raised. You will need some help in coming up with some healthy guidelines for disciplining your children. Parenting groups are a wonderful source for help with these sorts of problems.

Breaking the Cycle of Sexual Abuse

If you were sexually molested or abused, your abilities to feel empathy might be shut down, or you may still be in denial about the damage that was done to you. In either case, you may be at risk to sexually molest your children. You may also be inclined to close your eyes to the molestation of your children by your partner, or to the abuse of one of your children by another. Following are some questions to ask yourself to help you to recognize signs of sexual abuse in yourself or others:

Do you have dreams or fantasies about sexual involvement with your child?

Do you fear that you could sexually abuse your children?

Have you had impulses to sexually touch or caress your child during bathing or diapering?

Have you ever been afraid that your partner could sexually abuse your child?

Do you worry about how your partner or an older sibling embraces or holds your child?

Do you notice that your child or partner pays too much physical attention to your child?

Do you ever notice that an older child is being verbally abusive to a younger sibling?

Do you worry that an older child is spending too much time with a younger sibling?

Is your younger child afraid of an older sibling?

Is your younger child overly attached to an older sibling?

Understand that you are responsible for actions you take as an adult, even if those actions have their roots in your past as a victim of abuse. It is your duty as a parent to resist your impulse to molest your child. Therapy can help you to understand the causes behind these impulses, and will also help you to clear away any denial you might be experiencing regarding abuse of your children by others. You have the opportunity to stop the cycle of abuse and to give your children the chances you never had for a normal, healthy life. In so doing, you will continue to heal yourself.

Fostering Healthy and Open Communication

Most people do not grow up in homes where there is healthy and open communication. You and your sibling have had to learn how to talk to each other. Now it's time to teach your children to communicate in open, affectionate ways. Here are some guidelines for healthy communication in families:

Listen to your children and encourage them to listen to each other.

Respect your children's feelings. Encourage them to tell you and their siblings when they are upset or feel they are being treated unfairly.

Tell your children you love them.

Be physically affectionate with your children and encourage them to be physically affectionate with one another.

Encourage your children to work out their differences on their own by talking with each other about how they feel.

Encourage negotiation and compromise instead of threats, demands, name-calling, manipulation, or bullying.

Do not allow your children to abuse each other, physically or verbally.

Teach your children to respect one another's feelings. The best way to do that is for you and your partner to show that same respect.

As we've seen, you can change. You can change both yourself and your most important relationships. It's wonderful to see clients or friends who have conquered their pasts and are now having healthy relationships with their siblings and raising their own children free from the problems they had as kids.

My client Gloria described the satisfaction she feels at being able to break the cycle of abuse in her family. "My sister and I have both been able to love our kids and raise them in a healthy way, despite our own background, which really was pretty bad. I tell my kids I love them, something I never heard from my parents. My sister is extraordinarily patient with her two girls, another thing we never witnessed growing up. When we get together and watch our kids, sometimes we cry because we missed so much, but then we cry with joy because we have each other. We're doing a good job, and it's nurturing us to nurture our kids."

The foundations for a loving world are built within each family, but it is up to each of us to improve upon those foundations. Much of the value or meaning of life comes from the connections we make, first to ourselves and then to those around us. The more we understand ourselves and others, the more truthful and transcendent our lives become.

The big statements like "brotherhood of man" are really reducible to you, me, and our brothers and sisters. What we learn and do with each other, we do in the world. Learning to be the best brother or sister you can be will take you into the future with your sibling, equipped with the tools to make the world a better place.

Bibliography

Adler, Alfred. 1928. "Characteristics of First, Second and Third Children." *Children* 3 (Issue 5).

———. 1978. *Understanding Human Nature.* New York: Premier Books/Fawcett Publications.

Bank, Stephen, and Kahn, Michael D. 1975. "Sisterhood-Brotherhood Is Powerful: Sibling Sub-Systems and Family Therapy." *Family Process* 14 (September): 311–37.

———. 1982. *The Sibling Bond.* New York: Basic Books.

Bossard, J. H., and Boll, E. S. 1956. *The Large Family System.* Philadelphia: University of Pennsylvania Press.

Bowen, M. 1972. "Toward the Differentiation of Self in One's Own Family." In J. Framo (ed.), *Family Interaction: A Dialogue Between Therapists and Researchers.* New York: Springer, pp. 111–174.

Cicirelli, Victor G. 1985. "Sibling Relationships Throughout the Life Cycle." In Luciano L'Abate (ed.), *Handbook of Family Psychology and Therapy,* vol. 1. Homewood, IL: Dorsey Press, pp. 177–214.

Dunn, Judy, and Kendrick, Carole. 1982. *Siblings.* Washington, D.C.: Howard University Press.

Dunn, Judy, and Plomin, Robert. 1990. *Separate Lives: Why Siblings Are So Different.* New York: Basic Books.

Engel, Beverly. 1989. *The Right to Innocence: Healing the Trauma of Childhood Sexual Abuse.* Los Angeles: Tarcher.

Ferreira, A. J. 1963. "Family Myth and Homeostasis." *Archives of General Psychiatry* 9.

Gerstle, J. 1956. *Coalitions in the Sibling Triad.* Minneapolis: University of Minneapolis, Dept. of Sociology Mimeograph.

Hooper, M. M., and Harper, J. M. 1987. *Birth Order Roles and Sibling Patterns in Individual and Family Therapy.* Rockville, MD: Aspen Publishers.

Jackson, D. D. 1957. "The Question of Family Homeostasis." *Psychiatric Quarterly* 31 (Suppl.): 79–90.

Kahn, M. D., and Lewis, G. L. (eds.). 1988. *Siblings in Therapy.* New York: W. W. Norton & Co.

Lamb, Michael E., and Sutton-Smith, Brian (eds.). 1982. *Sibling Relationships: Their Nature and Significance Across the Lifespan.* NJ: Lawrence Erlbaum Associates.

Minuchin, S. 1974. *Families and Family Therapy.* Cambridge, MA: Harvard University Press.

Minuchin, S.; Mantalvo, B.; et al. 1967. *Families of the Slums.* New York: Basic Books.

Schachter, F. 1982. "Sibling De-identification and Split-Parent Identification: A Family Tetrad." In M. Lamb and B. Sutton-Smith (eds.), *Sibling Relationships: Their Nature and Significance Across the Lifespan.* NJ: Lawrence Erlbaum Associates.

Schachter, Frances F.; Shore, Ellen; Feldman-Rotman, Susan; Marquis, Rush; and Campbell, Susan. 1976. "Sibling De-identification." *Developmental Psychology* 12(5): 418–27.

Sutton-Smith, B., and Rosenberg, B. G. 1970. *The Sibling.* New York: Holt, Rinehart & Winston.

Toman, Walter. 1969. *Family Constellation.* New York: Springer.

Wiehe, Vernon R. 1990. *Sibling Abuse: Hidden Physical, Emotional, and Sexual Trauma.* Lexington, MA: Lexington Books.

Zuk, G. 1972. *Family Therapy: A Triadic-Based Approach.* New York: Behavioral Publications.

Index

Abuse, physical or emotional, 5, 9, 151–169
  anger and, 155–158
  avoiding repeating, with own children, 203–205
  co-dependent siblings and, 165–169
  getting help for, 204–205
  guilt or shame and, 155–156
  low self-esteem and, 159, 169
  parental encouragement of, 162–165
  self-blame for, 151–152
  from siblings, 152–153, 158–165
Abuse, sexual, 171–174
  avoiding cycle of, 205–206
  guilt or shame and, 173, 174
  recognizing signs of, 205–207
  self-blame for, 174
  by siblings, 174
Adult Children of Alcoholics, 168
Alcoholics Anonymous, 168
Alcoholism, parental, 56
  effects of, on family, 28–29
Alliances between siblings. *See also* Protector
    or rescuer role; Co-dependent siblings
  birth order and, 49–51
  exclusion from, 49–51
  resolving, 50, 51
  senselessness of, in adulthood, 49
Anger
  learning to dissipate, 157–158
  parental expectations and, 14
  physical or emotional abuse and, 155–158
Anxiety, as reaction to parents' expectations, 24
Assertiveness, lack of, in younger siblings, 52–54
Attention, parental
  competition for, 114–116
  resentment of, 4

Bank, Stephen, 172–173, 174
Birth order/birth order roles, 9
  parental stereotypes and, 36
  problems associated with, 37

sibling alliances based on, 49–51
troubled families and, 51–54
Black sheep of family
  blaming, 100–103
  siblings of, 100–103
Blaming
  of black sheep, 100–103
  of favored sibling, 93–97
  of self, 85–90
Boundaries, parent/child, 129
Bullying of younger siblings, 4

Caretakers, 132–139
Caretaking demands of parents, effects of, 51–54
Changing sibling relationships, 18–19, 22, 26–27, 30, 32–33, 40–41, 42–43, 46, 48, 51, 54, 56–57, 66, 69, 75–76, 79–80, 89–90, 92–93, 96–97, 99–100, 113–114, 116, 120, 126–127, 135–136, 138–139, 148–149, 157–158, 161–162, 164–165, 168–169, 195–196. *See also* *specific aspects of sibling relationships, e.g.,* Competition; Favoritism
Co-dependent siblings, 165–169
Codependents Anonymous (CODA), 167, 168
Communication, healthy, fostering with own children, 206–207
Competition, 8–9, 105–127. *See also* Sibling rivalry
  admitting feelings of, 123–124
  age difference and, 124
  for attention, 114–116
  backing away from, 4
  buried feelings of, 120–124
  defeated sibling in, 117–120
  denial of, 106
  dysfunctional families and, 124–125
  generation of, by parents, 108–116
  healthy, encouraging in own children, 199–201
  hidden, 106–107
  open, 107

211

parental, and familial labels, 77
for parental love and approval, 110–116
questions to ask self about, 107–108
sibling-generated, 116–117
unresolved feelings, 105–106
Conflict, parental, 9, 129–149
coping with, through compatible roles, 131–139
deflecting, 139–145
disruptive sibling roles in, 139–149
mediating of, by siblings, 132–136
siblings on opposite sides in, 145–149
Conflict resolution, healthy, teaching children, 198–199
Control, parental
children's reactions to, 23–24
labeling as means of, 73
Criticism, sensitivity to, 8

Defeated sibling, 117–120
Deflecting of parental conflicts, 139–145
Denial
of competition, 106
of sexual abuse, 205
Destructive relationships, avoiding, 5
Developmental stages, sibling's reaction to, 39
Dysfunctional families. See Families, dysfunctional

Emotional abuse. See Abuse, physical or emotional
Emotional characteristics of siblings, perceptions of, 37
Equalizing sibling relationships, 35–57
Expectations, parental, 9, 13–33
backfiring of, 23–24
differing, influence of on sibling relationships, 16–20
discovering, 24
and expectations of children, 20–22
power carried by, 14
removing obstacle of, for own children, 197–198
of stage mothers/fathers, 25–27
Expectations of siblings, parents' relationship and, 20–22

Familial labels. See also Labels/labeling, parental
siblings divided by, 77–80
use of, by parents, 76–80
Families, dysfunctional
and birth order roles, 51–54
black sheep in, 100–103
competition in, 109–111
incest in, 173–175
lack of competition in, 124–125
physical or emotional abuse in, 151–169
sibling's leaving home in, 54–56
Family myths
confronting, 30
effects of, on children, 29–30
power of, 27–30
and roles in family, 27–28
Family secrets, living with, 31–33
Favoritism, 5, 9. See also Sibling rivalry
assumptions based upon, 85
avoiding damaging children with, 201–202
effects of, on siblings, 5–6
blame of favored sibling and, 93–97
effects of, 87–89
effects of, on siblings, 81–103
lack of rational reasons for, 82–84
negative effects of, for favored child, 82
parents' reasons for, 82–83
questions to ask self about, 84–85
self-blame and, 85–90
self-image and, 86–87
sibling rivalry and, 97–100
use of, by favored siblings, 90–93
Feelings toward siblings, quiz on, 2
Friendships, effect of sibling relationship on, 6–7

Grandparents, favoritism shown by, 82, 83

Handicapped sibling, 73–76
Healthy sibling relationship, helping own children develop, 196–207

Inner-directedness, 107

Jealousy, 39, 106, 108. See also Competition; Power dynamics of sibling relationships

Kahn, Michael, 172–173, 174

Labels/labeling, parental, 59–80
  assumptions reflected by, 59
  avoiding, with own children, 202–203
  becoming aware of, 61–62
  familial traits and, 76–80
  getting beyond, 61–62
  harmful effects of, 60–61
  lopsided, effects of, 63–66
  as means of control, 73
  negative, effects of, 69–76
  positive, effects of, 66–69
  realistic, 60
  seeking reinforcement of, 60
  as self-fulfilling prophecies, 60–61
Limitations, own, discovering, 117
Love and approval of parents,
  competition for, 110–116

Manipulation of siblings, 46
Marriage
  effect of sibling relationship on, 5–6
  repetition compulsion and, 4–5
Myths, family
  confronting, 30
  effects of, on children, 29–30
  power of, 27–30
  and roles in family, 27–28
Myths, sibling, 41–43
  holding on to, 41–43
  protection stories, 41, 42

Name-calling, 70–73. See also Labels/labeling,
  parental: negative
Needs, parental, 9
  children as fulfillment of, 25–27
  children's awareness of, 14
  and parental expectations, 14, 17–18
Neglect. See Abuse, physical or emotional

Older sibling(s), 43. See also Younger sib-
  ling(s)
  dilemma of, 46–48
  parental role placed upon, 51–54
  power of, 47–48
  role of, 47, 48
  stereotypes of 35, 36

Older/younger sibling dynamic. See Power
  dynamics of sibling relationships

Parent-child roles, confusion of, 129–131
Parental conflict. See Conflict, parental
Parental relationships. See also Source relationships
  and expectations of siblings, 20–22
  as source relationships, 4
Parents. See also Families, dysfunctional
  expectations of (see Expectations,
    parental)
  favoritism of, 81–103
  identification with children, 108–109
  narcissistic interest in children's accom-
    plishments, 63–66
  narcissistic needs of, and favoritism, 83
  relationship needs of, 20–22
Perceptions of sibling, favoritism, and 86–87,
  89
Pleasing parent, competitiveness in, 110
Power dynamics of sibling relationships
  birth order and, 38–43
  equalizing, 43–57
  reactive responses and, 38–39
  work relationships and, 7–8
Problem-solving ability, lack of, and negative
  labeling, 70–73
Protection stories, retelling, 41
Protector or rescuer role, 42, 133–139,
  152–153, 165–169

Reactive responses, 39–43
  of adult siblings, 40–41
  age-related power discrepancies and,
    38–43
  entrenchment of, 38–43
Relationship needs, of parents, 20–22
Repetition compulsion, 5
  friendships and, 6–7
  marriage and, 5–6
  in relationship with children 8–9
  work relationships and, 7–8
Rescuer role. See Protector or rescuer role
Resentment, 4
  covering up feelings of, 7
  of older siblings, 52–54
  parental expectations and, 14